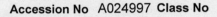

Student Support Materials for

OCR AS Sociology

Unit G671

Socialisation, Culture and Identity with Research Methods

Author: Fionnuala Swann
Series editor: Peter Langley

Published by Collins Education
An imprint of HarperCollins Publishers
77-85 Fulham Palace Road
Hammersmith
London
W6 8JB

Browse the complete Collins Education catalogue at
www.collinseducation.com

10 9 8 7 6 5 4 3 2 1

ISBN 978-0-00-741835-0

Fionnuala Swann asserts her moral right to be identified as the author of this work.

British Library Cataloguing in Publication Data.

A catalogue record for this publication is available from the British Library.

Commissioned by Charlie Evans and Andrew Campbell

Project editor: Sarah Vittachi

Design and typesetting by Hedgehog Publishing Limited

Cover Design by Angela English

Production by Simon Moore

Printed and bound by L.E.G.O. S.p.A Italy

Indexed by Indexing Specialists (UK) Ltd

Acknowledgements

Every effort has been made to contact the holders of copyright material, but if any have been inadvertently overlooked the publishers will be pleased to make the necessary arrangements at the first opportunity.

p8, source: Office for National Statistics; Bernard Crick et al., *The New and the Old: the report of the Life in the United Kingdom* (2003), Home Office; p22, source: Gerald Handel, *Children and Society: The Sociology of Children and Childhood Socialization* (2006), Oxford University Press; p28, source: Richard Jenkins, *Social Identity* (1997), Routledge; p35, source: Equality and Human Rights Commission; p49, © Yui Mok/PA Wire/ Press Association Images; p76, source: Teresa Tinklin, Linda Croxford, Alan Ducklin and Barbara Frame, 'Gender and Attitudes to Work and Family Roles: the Views of Young People at the Millennium', *Gender and Education* 17, (2005), Routledge, Available: http://www.informaworld.com/10.1080/0954025042000 301429; p83, source: Munira Mirza et al., *Living Apart Together: British Muslims and the Paradox of Multi-Culturalism* (2007), Policy Exchange.

Thanks to the following students for providing answers to the questions:

Ruby Barwood, Collette Blackman, Lauren Foley, Vicki Gill, Jessica Gowers, Fran Guratsky, Rachel Hewitt, Ella Keating, Charlotte Ross, Eric Wedge-Bull.

Contents

Contents

The formation of culture: key concepts

Culture

The term 'culture' can be summarized as the learned and shared way of life of any society. It includes a society's language, beliefs, **values** and **norms**, customs, dress, diet and the **roles**, which people use to make sense of their social world. Our culture provides us with guidelines and rules that help us to accomplish everyday activities and relate socially to other people.

The word 'culture' is often used interchangeably with the concept of 'society', but these two concepts do not mean the same thing. Culture is what forms the connection between the individual and society. It tells the individual how to operate effectively within social institutions that make up society – such as the family, the education system or the workplace. For example, many societies have an institution called the education system and it is a society's culture, which helps to provide guidelines for individuals to enable them to 'fit into' this institution. This is achieved through a cultural understanding of school norms and rules, the different roles that are performed, the customs, dress codes, expectations and so on.

Culture is made up of several different aspects, including values, norms, **status** and roles.

Values

Values are general principles or beliefs about what is desirable and worthwhile. Moral values refer to beliefs about what is right and wrong. These values provide general guidelines for behaviour and relate to ideals of what is viewed as important. Some values are seen as universal; for example, most societies place a high value on human life and good health.

Other values are relative and can differ between societies; for example, British values may include democracy, achievement, wealth and romantic love, but these are not necessarily shared with other societies.

Sociologists disagree on who decides a society's key values and in whose interests they operate. Functionalists argue that a shared agreement exists about our basic values and that these form the basis of a stable, ordered society. Marxist sociologists, however, argue that our values have been defined by the rich **ruling class**.

Norms

Norms are social rules that define the acceptable and expected ways of behaving in a given social situation. Norms are much more precise than values – they are essentially values put into practice; for example, the norm of knocking on a door before entering someone else's room or house reflects the value of privacy. Norms are specific to social situations; for example, laughing and dancing would be a norm associated with being at a nightclub but not at a funeral. In this sense, norms are relative.

Breaking norms would generally be seen as deviant behaviour and they are usually enforced using informal **sanctions** such as the disapproval of others, embarrassment or a 'telling off' from parents. When people break society's formal norms (laid down as laws), then the sanctions become more formal.

Customs are norms that have lasted for a long time and have become a part of society's traditions; for example, decorating a tree at Christmas time or buying presents for people's birthdays.

Status

The term status is used in two main ways. It can refer to the social position of people in society, such as a mother or a worker, or it can refer to the ranking of individuals. This ranking is determined by the prestige or respect attached to someone's position, given by other members of society. Status is therefore about people's social standing in the eyes of others.

Sociologists usually distinguish between two types of status: **ascribed status** (given at birth, which cannot be changed) and **achieved status** (usually through an individual's own efforts, skills and talent).

Roles

Roles are patterns of behaviour that are expected of a person or group of people in different positions in society. We all play many different roles in our lifetime – being a student, a sister or employee are all roles that bring with them certain expectations. For example, doctors are expected to act out their professional role, which is to be impartial, polite, scientific and so on. A teacher who fights, or a shopkeeper who gives his produce away, is clearly not following the expected behaviour associated with these roles.

Roles develop and change over a person's lifetime. Some roles are ascribed; for example, the role of a son or a brother; others, such as occupational roles, are achieved. As individuals take on many different roles, this may lead to role conflict, where successful performance of two or more roles at the same time may cause conflict and stress.

Essential notes

Notice the similarity between roles and status. The definitions are very similar, but an important difference is that status is about hierarchy (high and low status), whereas roles are about expected behaviour associated with a particular status.

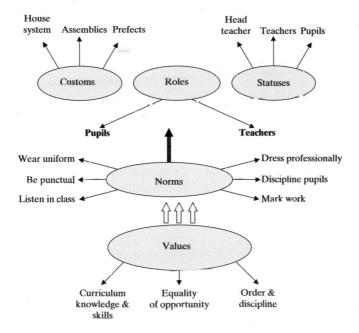

Fig 1
Linking the key concepts: schools

Types of cultures

High culture

High culture refers to the cultural practices that are associated with the powerful and wealthy elite or upper **social classes**. It is often contrasted with, and seen as superior to, **popular culture**, or culture of the masses.

In Britain, examples of high culture include entertainment such as opera, the theatre, fine art, classic literature and intellectual films. Supporters of high culture believe these activities are special because they represent the nation's cultural heritage. As well as being artistic and often expensive, these cultural products tend to require a high level of education on the part of the audience in order to appreciate their value. Some writers have described high culture as being superior to the culture of the masses. Sociologists influenced by Marxist views argue that the definition of high culture is determined by the ruling class. It is their tastes that decide what qualifies as culture.

Popular culture

Popular culture refers to the activities enjoyed by the masses, or the vast majority of ordinary people. Popular culture is dominated by mass-produced entertainment such as Hollywood films, soap operas on television and pop music. It is often contrasted in a negative way with high culture, and may be portrayed as shallow and meaningless. The literary critic F. R. Leavis feared that the mass media would lower the cultural standards of the population and turn people away from more intellectually demanding cultural forms such as classic English literature.

Dominic Strinati argues that the media are largely responsible for creating popular culture and they have manufactured it in order to make a profit. Consider, for example, the popular television series *The X Factor*. As well as watching the TV show, viewers can download individual songs immediately after the shows, buy a range of *X Factor* branded products such as books, magazines and pencil cases, and book to see *The X Factor* live tour.

Postmodernists see popular culture as an important development and argue that it increases people's choices with regard to lifestyles and identities.

However, Marxist sociologists view popular culture as harmful since it discourages critical thought. In this sense, it may be seen as the new 'opium of the masses'. Marxists also see popular culture as contributing to capitalism, as it essentially encourages consumerism. Other critical views of popular culture object to the way it is dominated by American culture such as Hollywood films and McDonald's restaurants.

High culture	Popular culture
Classical music	Pop, rock, soul, etc.
Shakespeare's plays	West End musicals
Intellectual foreign films	Hollywood blockbuster films
Art documentaries	Soap operas
The Sunday Times	*The Sun*
Booker Prize-winning novels	Best-selling romances and thrillers

Table 1
Examples of high culture and popular culture

Subculture

Subcultures are a minority part of the majority culture. Although they are committed to the wider culture that dominates society, they have distinct norms and values, which distinguish them as different. Examples of subcultures in the UK include youth subcultural groups such as 'goths' and 'emos', environmental/eco subcultural groups and religious subcultural groups, such as Scientologists. Some subcultural groups are based on leisure pursuits such as skaters or football fans. This range of subcultures in British society illustrates the fact that Britain is a culturally diverse society.

A range of sociological theories have focused on the role of subcultures, with attention given to deviant subcultural groups or school-based subcultural groups as sources of criminal or deviant behaviour and educational underachievement. For example, sociologists from the Birmingham Centre for Contemporary Cultural Studies, writing from a Marxist perspective, argue that youth subcultural groups such as skinheads, mods and punks resist capitalism, albeit in a symbolic way. Functionalist subcultural theorists have focused on the deficiencies of working-class culture as an explanation for juvenile delinquency.

Essential notes

The idea of subculture links to **cultural diversity** (see page 8).

Examiners' notes

All of the concepts relating to culture could be asked as an 8-mark concept question. Ensure that you learn a clear definition and two detailed examples for each one.

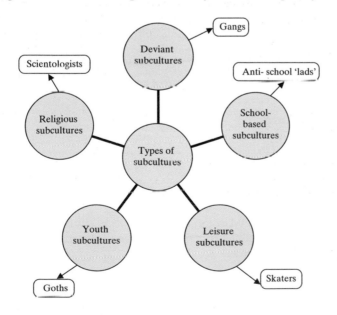

Fig 2
Examples of subcultures

This topic continues on the next two pages

Cultural diversity

The concept of cultural diversity relates to cultural differences within a society. It links to the idea of subcultures because the existence of different subcultures leads to a culturally diverse society. In the UK this diversification takes a number of different forms:

- Ethnic diversity – approximately 9% of the UK population is made up of minority ethnic groups who remain committed to aspects of their mother culture, such as language, food, customs and religion while subscribing to the norms and values of wider British culture.
- Social class diversity – Britain is a class society made up of different socio-economic groups – the upper class, middle class and working class. Each has its own distinctive cultural characteristics.
- Regional diversity – the key regions of the UK (Northern and Southern England, Scotland and Wales) each have their own traditions, customs and norms.
- Sexual diversity – the decriminalization of homosexuality and the liberalization of social attitudes, as well as sexual equality legislation, has led to the emergence of visible gay and lesbian subcultures and social scenes in most large British cities.
- Political diversity – in addition to the main parties, there are several political groups whose supporters reject the dominant centralist values. Environmental groups and anti-globalization groups tend to have such counter-cultural values.

Multiculturalism

Multiculturalism is the promotion of cultural diversity. The two concepts are closely related but multiculturalism specifically relates to promoting ethnic diversity. According to Bernard Crick, a multicultural society is *'made up of a diverse range of cultures and identities, with a need for a continuous process of mutual engagement and learning about these with respect, understanding and tolerance'*. In this sense, multiculturalism promotes the belief that different ethnic cultures can exist side by side and each group has the right to preserve its own cultural heritage. Multicultural policies aim to celebrate differences through, for example, multi-faith religious education and the celebration of a range of ethnically diverse festivals.

Consumer culture

Consumer culture is related to the goods and services we buy and consume in society. Over the last 30 years there has been increasing emphasis on consumption and it is generally agreed that we now live in a consumer society, where our identity is largely defined by what we buy and consume.

There are both cultural and economic aspects of consumer culture. Culturally, a consumer society portrays its sense of **identity** through the goods it consumes – from music and fashion to clothes and technology. Economically, a consumer culture is associated with a move away from manufacturing to a service-based economy; from production to consumption.

Essential notes

Policies promoting multiculturalism have come under attack recently with some politicians arguing that they don't work and that they actually create more tension between different ethnic communities.

Examiners' notes

It may be useful to do a newspaper search of articles about multiculturalism so that you can introduce some evaluative comments about such policies.

As the UK has transformed into a consumer culture, shopping has become a major leisure pursuit. In the last 10 years there have been four major developments that demonstrate the increased focus on shopping:

1. The increasing importance of **conspicuous consumption** – the buying of particular brands, logos and designer goods as status symbols, which is strongly encouraged by the advertising industry and endorsed by celebrities.
2. Investment in new shopping experiences such as extra-large supermarkets and out-of-town shopping centres.
3. The growth of internet shopping.
4. The easy availability of credit and loans.

Global culture

Global culture is the idea that, due to the development of social and economic relationships on a global scale, people all around the world are becoming part of one all-embracing culture. In other words, we all share a similar way of life. For example, we watch the same television programmes and films, drive the same cars and eat the same brand of pizza.

This progression towards 'sameness' is questioned by some critics who worry that such a homogenous mass entertainment culture will erode national and ethnic differences. They argue that global culture is, in fact, the spread of American culture. However, according to Mike Featherstone, there is no such thing as a universal global culture as people throughout the world do not share similar lifestyles. He does, however, believe that it is reasonable to talk of the 'globalization of culture', whereby some aspects of culture cross state boundaries and become widely dispersed across most areas of the world.

Giddens discusses the various forces that help create a global culture. These include:

- Television: brings British, and especially American, culture into homes throughout the world daily.
- A global economy: businesses, factories, management structures, markets and finance often span continents and countries.
- Global citizens: managers of large corporations, sports stars or entertainers may spend as much time travelling the globe as they do at home.
- International organizations such as the United Nations agencies, multinational banks and the World Health Organization.
- Electronic communication: telephone, email, the internet and the World Wide Web.

Essential notes

Notice how all these concepts are very closely linked. For example, global culture is very similar to mass or popular culture but on a bigger scale. Global culture is also linked to consumer culture, as is popular culture. It is worth being aware of the links between the concepts as you can use these as an opportunity to introduce more concepts in a written examination answer.

Examiners' notes

You will not be asked a specific theoretical question in the exam because theory isn't explicitly on the specification. You can, however, incorporate theory into a question on culture as it demonstrates a wider and deeper knowledge and understanding, as well as critical evaluation.

Examiners' notes

These are good criticisms to learn, as they are general criticisms of functionalism and can be applied to a range of different topic areas. For example, when discussing how agencies of socialization socialize individuals, you can make the evaluative comment that individuals are not passive beings who merely accept the socialization process without question.

Theories of culture

Functionalism and culture

Émile Durkheim (1858–1917), the founder of functionalism, argued that society exists above the individual and that people's behaviour is shaped by social forces. He argued that our sense of culture and identity is the result of being socialized into a modern society. We learn norms, values and an entire set of cultural perceptions from our society, and these enable us to share ways of thinking and behaving with the rest of society. Durkheim described these shared ways of thinking as the **collective conscience** of society.

Functionalists argue that in order for societies to exist, there must be a shared sense of social order. Without this, societies would disintegrate into chaos and anarchy. Durkheim was particularly concerned with explaining how social order in society is maintained, especially in modern industrial societies, which are complex and more individualistic than pre-industrial societies. His answer was that societies need to be based on **value consensus** – shared agreement about what is worthwhile and desirable. The function, or role, of social institutions such as the family, education and religion is to socialize individuals into this value consensus.

Functionalists see culture as important in maintaining value consensus. It acts as a bonding 'glue', holding the various parts of society together and enabling them to function effectively.

Criticisms of functionalism

- Functionalists tend to neglect conflict – culture does not always act as a social glue, as the many conflicts over cultural differences demonstrate.
- Functionalists ignore the role of individuals in shaping culture. Interactionist sociologists argue that individuals are not passive beings who merely accept the socialization process without question. Rather, individuals are reflexive thinking beings who have freedom to make choices and decisions.

Marxism and culture

Karl Marx (1818–83) argued that all human societies are economically based; they are organized to provide for their members' material needs such as food, clothing and shelter.

For Marx, a society's culture is simply a reflection of the kind of economic system that provides for these material needs. He argued that the economic systems of all societies have given rise to class relationships. This is because in most societies one class of people (the ruling class) has taken control of the way in which the economy is organized and has exploited the remainder of society (the **subject class**) to carry out the production. This creates an inevitable conflict of interest between the two classes.

Marx saw this conflict as an inevitable and basic feature of capitalist societies, which would eventually lead to the overthrow of capitalism. He then explained the ability of capitalist societies to survive for so long with the concept of **ideology**. Marx described ideology as the ideas of the ruling class that help to legitimize and justify the existing economic system. In other words, cultural ideas and values are dominated by ruling-class ideas and values. He argued that the role of social institutions such as the family, the education system and the media was to socialize the working class into accepting ruling-class culture.

Another aspect of Marx's work, which relates to the study of culture is his concept of **commodification**. Marx argued that in capitalist societies, products increasingly become commodities – things that can be bought and sold. The mass media, and advertising in particular, play an important part in this. Advertising convinces people that they need more and more things produced by capitalism. According to Marx, this creates false needs and helps to divert attention away from the contradictions and exploitation inherent in capitalism.

Marx used the term **commodity fetishism** to describe the attitude towards commodities in capitalist societies where people worship consumer goods. For example, when a young person spends hundreds of pounds on a pair of the latest 'must have' designer trainers, the shoes are like fetishes to be worshipped.

Examiners' notes

These concepts (highlighted in bold) underpin the basic functionalist and Marxist theories. It is important that you understand the flavour of each theory so that you are able to apply this understanding to the concept of culture.

Essential notes

These concepts (highlighted in bold) can be linked to consumer culture. The increasing emphasis on buying 'must have' goods inevitably leads to the development of a consumer culture.

Functionalism	Marxism
Shopping is a cultural norm in contemporary society. • It functions to help the economy in terms of promoting business. A booming economy is beneficial for the whole of society. • The social activity of shopping fosters a sense of social cohesion and solidarity and therefore helps to promote stability in society	Shopping is an activity that benefits the ruling class. It does this on two main levels: • It is an example of commodification, which promotes capitalism and the pursuit of profits. • The ideological role of shopping is that false needs are created, which encourage people to focus their thoughts on which pair of shoes to buy rather than the fact they are being exploited in a capitalist system.

Table 2
Theoretical explanations of culture: shopping as an example

Criticisms of Marxism

- Some critics feel that Marx placed too much emphasis on the role of economic structures in shaping other aspects of society such as ideas and beliefs.
- Marx may have overemphasized social class as the main source of conflict in society. Gender, religion and **ethnicity** may all be just as important as sources of conflict and inequality.

The process of socialization

Socialization is the process of learning society's culture. It is how individuals become skilled and competent members of society. Socialization involves learning the norms and values of a culture to the extent that the ways of thinking and behaving, which are accepted by that culture come to appear normal, natural and inevitable.

The first few years of a person's life are crucial to learning how to behave. However, it is important to understand that socialization is a life-long, continuous process. This is because, unlike animals, humans live in complex societies where interaction with others is negotiated using a sophisticated understanding of social rules. These need to be continually learned and reinforced.

There are a few rare and extreme examples that illustrate the importance of the process of socialization in the early years. These are case studies of **feral children**, who have grown up with limited human contact, either because they have been neglected by their families or, in some extreme cases, raised by animals. **Table 3** outlines some examples of the most unusual cases.

Table 3
Examples of feral children

Example	Absence of socialization	Description of feral behaviour
Isabelle	Spent most of her time up until the age of six in a dark room with her deaf and mute mother.	She could not talk; she only grunted. She could not walk properly. Her behaviour towards strangers was like a wild animal.
Horst	A young boy in Germany who was abandoned every day by his parents, who left him in the sole company of a female Alsatian dog.	Horst exhibited dog-like behaviour. He cocked up his leg, ate raw meat, howled like a dog and crawled around on all fours.
Kamala & Amala	Young twin girls who had been lost in the jungle in India and, when found, were living with wolves in a cave-like den.	The girls behaved like animals; they moved like the wolves; they were afraid of artificial light. They were scared of humans and they used no language to communicate.

These case studies of feral children illustrate the importance of early socialization. They indicate that without human contact, individuals do not learn the basic characteristics and behaviours, which we associate with being human. The extent to which individuals are born with natural, biological behaviour traits is a contested topic that has become known as the **nature–nurture debate**.

The nature–nurture debate

There are two opposing views on the key factors that shape our actions:

1. The biological view (nature): people are born with natural desires and uncontrollable instincts. Many features of being human are ascribed biologically. For example:

- when women cuddle babies, it is a result of their maternal instincts
- when men rape women, it is a result of their uncontrollable sexual desires
- when people go to war, it is the consequence of our naturally aggressive behaviour.

2. The sociological view (nurture): people's behaviour is socially learned. Desires, attitudes and patterns of behaviour vary tremendously from one society to another. The vast majority of human behaviour is learned through the process of socialization. For example:

- language is socially created – if babies are not spoken to, they will not be able to speak a language
- sexual violence and rape is a consequence of the way men learn that women are sexual objects, to be taken and used at will.

Social control

Social control is the term given to the various methods used to persuade or force individuals to conform to the dominant social norms and values of a society. Social control acts as a reminder to people about how they should behave in specific social situations. It also acts to prevent deviance, which is where individuals do not conform to society's norms.

There are two main mechanisms of social control, which back up the socialization process:

1. **Formal social control** – these mechanisms involve written rules, laws or codes of conduct that individuals need to follow. A system of sanctions such as prisons or fines, is created for people who deviate from these rules. Formal agencies of social control include the police, the courts, prisons, social services and the education system. There are also formal mechanisms of praising people when they perform particularly well in terms of meeting society's values and norms.
2. **Informal social control** – refers to the unwritten, more informal, ways of controlling people that we learn during everyday interactions. The family, media and **peer groups** all exercise control but without written rules and formal codes of conduct. Instead, they use informal ways of reinforcing behaviour.

Sanctions are the rewards and punishments by which social control is achieved and conformity to norms and values is enforced. These may be positive sanctions (rewards) or negative sanctions (punishments).

	Formal social control	Informal social control
Positive sanctions	Certificates of merit Knighthood Medal of honour	Smiling Clapping Reward charts
Negative sanctions	Prison Fines School exclusion	Being ignored Being grounded Being 'told off'

Essential notes

Social control and socialization act together to ensure that people follow society's culture. Socialization is the learning of society's values, norms and rules, and social control ensures that people abide by what they have learned.

Examiners' notes

The concepts of socialization and social control are closely linked, but make sure you know the difference between them. Many students make the mistake of discussing agencies of socialization without actually explaining the link to social control.

Sociological theories and socialization

There are two main types of socialization: primary and secondary.

Primary socialization

This is the earliest stage of socialization. It begins at birth and continues during the early years of a child's life. Most **primary socialization** takes place within the family and is very important in helping to shape human beings, as it involves learning basic social skills.

Another element in the definition of primary socialization is that it occurs between the individual and those people with whom they have primary (close, personal, intimate and face-to-face) relationships.

Secondary socialization

Secondary socialization starts when children begin to become more independent, usually when they enter the education system. This is the socialization that occurs between the individual and those people with whom they have secondary relationships.

The function of secondary socialization is to build on what has been learned in primary socialization so that children learn to understand and participate in the wider society, beyond their immediate family. According to Parsons, one of the main purposes (functions) of secondary socialization is to *'liberate the individual from a dependence upon the primary attachment and relationships formed within the family group'*.

The main agencies of secondary socialization are education, the mass media, the peer group, the workplace and religion.

Functionalist theory of the role of socialization

Functionalists argue that society is held together and avoids breakdown through the creation of a value consensus. All members of society need to learn the same core values and they do this through socialization. The individual then internalizes society's values so that they become part of her or his personality.

Everyone benefits from the socialization of people in accordance with these core values, as it ensures that people's behaviour becomes predictable, which contributes to the maintenance of social order.

The most important agency of socialization is the family. According to Parsons, the child in the family is like an empty vessel, which must be filled with shared cultural values and norms. This ensures that the child is committed to society's value consensus and so feels a strong sense of belonging to society.

Social control is also necessary and beneficial to all. It ensures that people are correctly socialized into society's norms and values. It ensures that dysfunctions are dealt with quickly and that there is a swift return to equilibrium when someone disobeys the rules.

Criticisms of the functionalist view

- Functionalists underestimate the amount of conflict that can take place in the process of socialization. For example, Gouldner argues that 'training children can be a continual ... battle.'

Examiners' notes

You should be able to make links between primary socialization and the nature–nurture debate using examples relating to feral children.

Essential notes

The role of the different agencies of socialization differs between societies and over time. For example, the education system and the mass media have become more significant in reinforcing socialization, whereas religion has, arguably, lost some of its significance.

- Functionalists fail to recognize that people don't always readily conform to the rules; deviating from social norms and values is commonplace. In this sense, functionalists present what Dennis Wrong described as an 'over-socialized view of man'.
- Many sociologists criticize the view of seeing children as 'empty vessels' that are simply filled with values and norms passed down to them. Children can play an active part in their own development.

Marxist theory of the role of socialization

Marxists argue that socialization involves the population being programmed into believing the values of the ruling class. Zaretsky, for example, argues that the family is used by the capitalist class to instil values such as respect for authority, which means that individuals can be exploited more easily in later life.

Unlike functionalists, who assume that everyone benefits from socialization, Marxists believe that only the ruling class benefits. Socialization is part of ruling-class ideology, which maintains and promotes the exploitation of the subject class.

Social control is used by the powerful in society to force or persuade the less powerful to behave as they want them to. For example, for Marxists, capitalism creates crime by creating vast social inequalities and promoting greed. Then, when working-class individuals commit crimes such as theft, they are severely punished by the police and judiciary. The blame is placed on the individual and never the capitalist system.

Criticisms of Marxism

Like functionalists, Marxists have been criticized for having an 'over-socialized' view of individuals and underestimating the level of conflict in the socialization process.

Examiners' notes

A basic understanding of the main theories can be applied to any example, from socialization or social control in general to the more specific examples of the role of the family or the education system. This 'theoretical thinking' is a useful skill to develop.

Examiners' notes

Including theory in your exam answers is a good way of picking up more marks for knowledge and understanding.

Examiners' notes

Theoretical criticisms are a useful way of demonstrating the skill of evaluation when a question requires you to evaluate a view or statement.

Functionalism	Marxism
Talcott Parsons	David Cooper
Socialization in the family takes place primarily through identification with adults	The family is an 'ideological conditioning device', which socializes children into accepting their own exploitation
Children imitate their parents, particularly in terms of **gender roles**	Children learn to obey their parents, just as they will obey employers in later life
Girls learn the expressive, emotional roles from their mothers	They are taught to play specific roles; for example, son or daughter, male or female
Boys learn the instrumental and breadwinner roles from their fathers	Such roles are restrictive and constraining; they limit the development of the 'self' and lay the groundwork for future indoctrination at school and in society generally

Table 4
An example of theoretical approaches to socialization within the family

The family and socialization

The main agency of primary socialization is the family. Examples of the behaviour of feral children on page 12 show that the first few years of socialization in the family are crucial to individuals learning to be human. Close and personal family relationships are essential for children to develop a sense of themselves as 'social beings'; to learn how to interact and communicate with other people. Through the process of primary socialization, children learn skills that are specific to humans: they learn emotional responses such as love, sadness and humour and they learn how to empathize with others.

Ways in which children learn the culture of their society

Manipulation: The way in which parents encourage and reward behaviour that they think is appropriate or discourage that which they think is inappropriate. A good example of this is in relation to gender-role socialization where, for example, parents may encourage their daughters to pay a lot of attention to their appearance and their sons to support football.

Language: The words and names that parents use when speaking to their children to teach them society's expectations. For example, girls are more likely to be called 'pretty' and 'princess', whereas boys are more likely to be told that they are a 'brave solider'. Oakley referred to these types of labels in relation to gender-role socialization as 'verbal appellations'.

Expectations: Parents' hopes for their children can influence their expectation of future suitable careers. For example, some parents of children who have been labelled as exceptionally gifted and talented have directed them to involvement in challenging academic activities from a very young age.

Activities: Parents provide children with a whole range of activities, toys and games through which they learn about their wider culture. For example, they can learn the value of money through playing board games such as Monopoly; or the value of team work by playing family games such as Pictionary. Of course, by playing games, children are also being socialized into the values of competition and achievement.

Role model: Children learn the social roles expected of them by looking at role models within the family unit. For example, they will see their parents interacting with close friends or meeting new people and they learn the social norms associated with this.

Imitation: By copying the behaviour of adults, children are learning about role taking. Activities such as playing 'house' or 'mummies and daddies' develop skills of empathy as children gradually learn what it might feel like to be a parent. Basic norms such as how to eat, use the toilet, dress appropriately and manners at mealtimes are all learned through imitation.

Identification: Children can think of someone they admire and pretend to be them. Dressing-up costumes are very popular as children enjoy pretending to be characters such as Batman or Snow White. They are also learning important messages about gender identity through doing this.

Social control: The socialization process is often reinforced with the use of social control. Parents may use various positive and negative sanctions such as praising a child when they behave in an appropriate way. For example, children may get pocket money or stickers or treats as a reward. Negative sanctions are used to discourage inappropriate behaviour. For example, if children are rude to their parents they may be banned from watching television or have to do extra jobs around the house.

Theoretical explanations of the family as an agency of socialization

Functionalists

Functionalists see the family as a 'personality factory' where the child is a 'blank slate' at birth, and the role of parents is to mould and train the passive child to become an accepted member of society.

The child needs to be socialized into society's key norms and values to enable them to feel a strong sense of belonging to society. This socialization takes place mainly through identification with adults.

Parsons believed that it is beneficial to society if women take primary responsibility for childcare, while men are the main breadwinners. Therefore, part of socialization involves learning different gender roles in which women are more expressive (or emotional) and men are more instrumental (planning rationally to achieve certain goals).

Marxists

Marxists point out that the family teaches children about submitting to authority and being obedient. These are qualities that will be beneficial to the capitalist ruling class when children grow up and become employees.

They argue that children are socialized into being conforming members of society, but this does not benefit society as a whole; it benefits the capitalist ruling class.

Evaluation of the family as an agency of socialization

It is assumed that parents are successful agents in socializing children. However, not all adults acquire the skills that are required to nurture children and there are many examples of poor parenting and child neglect.

Some commentators suggest that childhood socialization is not as effective as it was in the past. Palmer (2007) notes that parents no longer spend enough quality time with their children – instead relying on 'electronic babysitters', which produce a 'toxic childhood'.

Essential notes

You should revise the theoretical explanations in conjunction with the more detailed section on theory on pages 10–11. Once you have a basic understanding of the theories, you can apply them to any agency of socialization.

Education and socialization

Children spend at least 11 years of their lives in compulsory schooling from the age of four or five, so the education system is one of the main agencies of secondary socialization.

Starting full-time school means that children have to learn to adapt to a new set of rules and norms. There are two main processes of social learning in operation at all schools – the **formal curriculum** and the **hidden curriculum**.

The formal curriculum

This refers to the official curriculum. Children are taught core skills needed in adult life, such as numeracy and literacy, from an early age. Much of the official school curriculum reflects wider values; for example, the presence of P.E. on the curriculum reflects the value society places on good health and fitness.

The formal curriculum also indicates which aspects of learning are seen as most important in socializing children. For example, in the UK, the foundation subjects of literacy, numeracy and science are seen as key, and a large part of curriculum time is devoted to teaching and learning them. Critics often question why these subjects are regarded as crucially important. They question why, for example, the teaching of modern foreign languages is not compulsory in an increasingly globalized society.

The national curriculum is important not only in teaching students knowledge and skills needed in adult life, but also in transmitting culture. In subjects such as history, religious education, English literature and art, aspects of culture are passed on. Some critics have described the national curriculum as ethnocentric, which means that it teaches British values and culture as being superior to others.

The hidden curriculum

This is also known as the informal curriculum and refers to the transmission of norms and values that are not part of the formal or official curriculum. The everyday rules, regulations and interactions of school life deliver lessons on how society functions. The hidden curriculum can also refer to the process of learning.

Unlike the formal curriculum, where the learning content is written down and delivered by teachers, students learn the messages of the hidden curriculum from informal interaction with others. What students learn is not formally taught to them, but in this way the rules and culture of the school are passed on.

Features of the hidden curriculum and what is being taught

- Privileges and responsibilities for sixth formers → respect for elders
- School rules, detentions and exclusions, rewards such as merit badges and prizes → conformity to society's rules and laws
- Competitive sports and class competition → value of competition
- Standing when teacher enters classroom → respect for authority

Essential notes

The term 'hidden curriculum' is essentially a Marxist concept, introduced by Bowles and Gintis to explain how schools prepare young people to be effectively exploited when they enter the workforce.

- Punctuality → value of time-keeping
- Grading by ability and exam success or failure → value of meritocracy – everyone making it to the top if she or he tries hard enough

Education processes and socialization

The processes by which children learn in school are, in some ways, similar to how they learn in the family (see page 16).

- Manipulation: Teachers will encourage appropriate behaviour, such as completing homework.
- Activities (canalization): Children's interests are directed into certain toys and play activities; for example, boys may be encouraged to play football at play times, whereas girls play 'house'.
- Role models: As well as teachers acting as role models, lessons include role models of historical figures (for example, Florence Nightingale) that encourage children to develop specific values.
- Imitation: Children are keen to 'fit in' at school and will often copy the behaviour of other students to ensure that they do so.
- Positive and negative sanctions: These are used to reward good behaviour or to punish bad behaviour.

Theoretical explanations of education as an agent of socialization
Functionalism

Functionalists believe that education systems are essential in that they transmit shared cultural values, which produces conformity and consensus. Education acts as a bridge between the family unit and wider society, preparing young people for the world of work. It socializes children into important values such as achievement, competition and individualism.

Subjects such as history, literature and language study and religious education link the individual to society, past and present, by encouraging a sense of pride. This reinforces a sense of belonging to society.

Marxism

In contrast to the functionalist viewpoint, Marxists argue that education is dominated by a hidden curriculum – a ruling-class ideology that encourages conformity and an unquestioning acceptance of the organization of the capitalist system. Schools therefore socialize students into uncritical acceptance of hierarchy, obedience and failure, which inevitably benefits capitalism.

Furthermore, the focus on competition and individual achievement discourages people from working collaboratively to achieve results that will benefit everyone equally or, in other words, working towards 'the common good' of all people.

The media and socialization

The media, or mass media, is arguably an increasing influence on the shaping of our norms and values. This includes newspapers, magazines, television, films and the internet.

Many people access the mass media to interpret and make sense of the world around them as they usually have very little direct experience of the events portrayed. Therefore, media images and messages can be very powerful in shaping the views and opinions of those who are exposed to it.

Table 5 provides some examples of the link between what the media is used for and the type of communications channel this may correspond to.

The purpose of the mass media	Communications channel
To provide information about what is happening in the world	Newspapers, television news, news websites
To communicate with others	Mobile phones, internet (e.g. social networking sites), email
To promote the image of products to increase sales	Advertising in newspapers, magazines and posters, on television, radio, online
To offer escapism into fiction as a leisure activity	Television (e.g. soap operas), films, books

Table 5
Mass media: purpose and channels

The role of the media in socialization

The media socializes individuals in a variety of ways:

- Role models: The media provides us with role models, which may help to reinforce socially acceptable ways of behaving and therefore act as a form of social control. In particular, in young children's television programmes and books, fictional characters are often portrayed as making morally right decisions and actions. For example, Peppa Pig feels much better sharing her toys with her brother rather than keeping them to herself.
- It has been argued that the media do not provide a varied enough range of positive role models, particularly for young women. Abi Moore, creator of the website 'PinkStinks', argues that 'young women desperately need role models – and what the media gives them is heiresses, sex objects, surgery addicts and emotional wrecks.'
- Representation of social groups: The media are inevitably selective and this may lead to a biased or stereotypical representation of social groups. For example, Ferguson found that women's magazines operated around a 'cult of **femininity**' and McRobbie criticized girls' magazines for their representation of femininity, centering around 'slimblondness'. (See page 32 for a discussion of the media and gender-role socialization.)
- Imitation: There are numerous examples of individuals being influenced by the media so much that they copy what they have seen, heard or read. These are commonly referred to as 'copycat' incidents. For example, Emo music has been accused of encouraging

young people to self-harm, and there is a long-running political debate about how watching violent films may lead to an increase in actual violent incidents.

- Consumer culture: The media plays an important role in creating and reinforcing a consumer culture. Through advertising, the media provides us with designs for living; images and ideas, which we use to fashion our identities. Consumer brands are often endorsed by celebrity role models, as the advertising industry believes that this can boost sales. Take, for example, a 20-second butter advert featuring John Lydon, a member of the 1970s punk band the Sex Pistols. The butter company claims that sales soared by 85% in the quarter after the advert was first aired on television.

Media effects

There is debate within the sociology of the media with regard to how influential the media is in shaping the thoughts and beliefs of individuals.

Early models of media effects suggest that the media has a direct and powerful effect on its audience, just as a drug would have a noticeable and immediate effect. This was known as the hypodermic model. Other theories suggest that this view is too simplistic; that media effects are probably more of a build-up over time (the drip-drip effect).

More recent theories suggest that people interpret media messages in different ways, and argue that there is no evidence that audiences passively accept what is being fed to them. Instead, audiences are selective and critical in their use of the media, using it to enhance their lives and identities.

Theoretical explanations of the role of the media in socialization
Marxism

Marxists argue that the mass media is responsible for the spread of mass or popular culture, which 'is devised and packaged by capitalism to keep the masses content' (Marsh and Keating, 2006). The media supports capitalism in two main ways:

1. It encourages 'false needs' (see page 11) through advertising, which acts to support capitalist enterprise.
2. It discourages any critical thoughts, particularly those that relate to questioning capitalism, through focusing on dumbed-down light entertainment, which produces superficial, mindless distraction.

Essential notes

Marxists argue that the mass media contributes to the ideological control of the working class. In this sense, the role of the media is to ensure that the working class do not question the exploitation and oppression caused by capitalism.

The peer group and socialization

Peer groups consist of people of a similar status who come into regular contact with one another such as groups of friends, school children in the same year or colleagues in the same job.

The peer group is an agency of secondary socialization and is, arguably, most influential for young people during adolescence. Peers are important agents of socialization since so much time is spent in school together.

Key study

Gerald Handel: An interactionist viewpoint

Gerald Handel (2006) outlines the process of socialization from an interactionist viewpoint. He argues that in the peer group, 'a child learns to function more independently, to acquire and test skills and beliefs that earn him a place among people of the same generation, to develop new outlooks that reflect youthful interests rather than adult interests.'

Differences in socialization

Table 6 shows the difference between socialization by adults (in the family) and socialization in peer groups (between children).

Socialization by adults	Peer group socialization
Socialization of children into common or core values	Provides an alternative to adult standards and may have different values
	Can lead to socialization conflict when the demands of the peer group contradict rules that derive from parental authority
Socialization for long-term adjustment to society	Concerned more with immediate gratification and inclusion within the peer group
Children follow rules passed down to them; clear sense of hierarchy	Children actively take part in making the rules – the culture and norms of behaviour develop in the course of interaction rather than being imposed from above

Table 6
Socialization of children by adults and peer groups

Even in adult life, peer groups are important in defining **norms** of behaviour. In professional occupations this may be formalized through professional associations, which train their members and set standards of entry. In most occupations, peer group control is more informal. For example, in a factory there may be an informal agreement between workers about how much work should be done in a shift. If workers attempt to exceed this they may be ostracized in order to encourage group conformity.

Peer group socialization

Peer groups act as an agency of socialization in the following ways:

- Different activities: Children often learn the rules of games and sports via peer groups rather than from formal sports lessons. This can also impact on gender-role socialization. For example, Skelton and Francis noted how playground space in primary schools is dominated by boys playing football, whereas girls are found at the margins, playing skipping games or talking.

- Resistance and rebellion: Youth is a time when rules are questioned and tested. Resisting established norms and values is generally accepted to be part of growing up and the peer group offers an expression of individuality that may be difficult to find elsewhere. Some youth subcultures, such as punks and skinheads, are based on rebellion and resisting the norm and, consequently, these groups come to be seen as deviant subcultures.

- **Peer group pressure**: Peer groups can exert pressure on individuals to imitate group behaviour. Belonging to and being accepted by a peer group are powerful forces, which encourage people to conform to group behaviour. This peer group pressure can be positive or negative. For example, it could encourage individuals to lead a healthy lifestyle by being sporty, or it could encourage unhealthy behaviour such as smoking. Failure to conform to the group's norms can lead to rejection and isolation and this makes it a powerful aspect of the socialization process.

- Learning about hierarchy: Peer groups often consist of individuals who have a higher status and who act as role models to others.

- Recognizing similarity: Peer groups are usually based around a similar interest; for example, a scouting or Girl Guide group, or members of a band. Sewell (2000) uses the term 'cultural comfort zones' to describe how peer groups tend to include people from similar social backgrounds. For example, in schools that are characterized by cultural diversity, students often group themselves according to their ethnic identities when they are in informal settings such as the canteen or common room. Cultural comfort zones suggest that peer groups form around a perceived central common trait.

Sociological theory and peer group socialization

Interactionists such as Handel (see key study), do not see socialization as a passive process in which children simply learn what they are taught and adults teach children to follow agreed norms and values. Nor do they believe that socialization involves learning a single, universally shared **culture** of society – deviant youth subcultures indicate that there can be alternative views.

Handel notes that childhood socialization can be viewed from two perspectives:

1. The socialization agents – such as parents and teachers.
2. The child who is being socialized – the agents of socialization are just one influence; they are also strongly influenced by peer groups, in which they socialize each other.

Examiners' notes

The use of relevant contemporary examples to illustrate a point is an acceptable way of gaining marks for knowledge and understanding.

Essential notes

The theory focused on here is **interactionism** or social action theory. This theory can be used as a general criticism of the process of socialization as it points out that children are not passive 'puppets' but active agents, involved in creating and recreating their socialization experiences.

The workplace and socialization

The workplace, as an agency of secondary socialization, is part of the continuous socialization process, which we experience throughout our lives. When people enter the workforce they have to be introduced to the skills, norms and values attached to the specific job. It may involve the following forms of learning:

- **Anticipatory socialization**: People may have learned something about the job beforehand, possibly by talking to people about it or taking a course in preparation.
- **Re-socialization**: When individuals start at a new place of work they have to learn new rules, regulations and **norms** of behaving. These include submitting to workplace discipline (such as regular work hours and obeying the boss) as well as learning the role for which they have been employed. This type of re-socialization occurs again when we move jobs because organizations vary in their styles and traditions.

Agents of workplace socialization include bosses, colleagues and even customers. Some of these agents socialize us in formal ways while others socialize us in more informal ways:

- **Formal socialization**: The management of a company takes formal responsibility for socializing employees. For example, they may provide training courses to develop the necessary work skills and mentors to help new workers to settle in. In addition, they usually lay down norms and rules about appearance, attitudes and behaviour. Some workplaces impose strict dress codes (such as shirt and tie for men). Behaviour may be controlled by official codes of conduct (for example, rules about accessing social networking sites during work time). Many firms also try to win the loyalty and motivation of their staff by encouraging them to identify with the company (for example, by offering them a substantial discount on their products).
- **Informal socialization**: This is the socialization provided by peer groups at work, as they introduce new workers to the informal culture of the workplace. The unwritten rules of the workplace are learned through observing others or through casual discussions with work colleagues. Workplace peer groups may have their own rituals such as playing jokes on newcomers. They may also have their own norms, many of which may not be approved by management. For example, they may try to slow down the pace of work – any colleague who works too hard is likely to be bullied or mocked, demonstrating the use of informal social control mechanisms.

Essential notes

Workplaces socialize people through the same processes as the other agencies of socialization. Individuals learn about how to 'survive' in the workplace and what they need to do through imitation, role models, peer pressure and social control.

Key study

Waddington: Informal socialization within the police force

Waddington (1999) carried out research into the informal culture of the police force. He argued that the 'canteen culture' they involved themselves in acts to socialize the police officers. He found that as police officers 'hang around' the station after work and spend their off-duty time together, they learn from listening to others telling their stories about how they overcame tricky situations and they also pick up practical tips and advice about surviving as a police officer. Waddington argues that this 'canteen culture' actually helps police officers deal with their stressful job in the following ways:

- It boosts their occupational self-esteem by giving them a 'heroic' identity (police officers have a hard job facing tough and often violent criminals).
- It reinforces their sense of 'mission' (they are doing a valuable job by fighting crime).
- It celebrates certain values that are more or less essential in police work (such as a 'macho' emphasis on physical strength and courage).

Examiners' notes

Note that the workplace can be compared to the school, where there is a formal curriculum (rules, training courses and so on) and an informal or hidden curriculum (which you learn from but are not actually taught).

Sociological theory and workplace socialization

Marxists argue that workers are socialized in a way that contributes to their continued exploitation at work, while also masking the true extent of this. For example, according to Ritzer (2002), young people often get their first experience of work in 'McJobs' – unskilled, low paid, part-time jobs in fast-food restaurants. Here, they are trained to perform simple tasks in a predictable manner, doing each action in exactly the same way. They have little scope for using their own initiative, and thus are unlikely to question authority or their low work position. Workers in such jobs are, in effect, turned into robots where even what they say and how they speak to customers is tightly controlled by management.

Essential notes

Berger and Luckmann can be linked to social action theories, as they focus on how individuals interpret and make sense of religion to aid their understanding of the world.

Religion and socialization

Religion is, arguably, a major institution in most societies, although it is often noted that in a culturally diverse society such as the UK there are a range of different religious groups and faiths.

In traditional societies, religious beliefs often form a central part of the **culture** of a society. In such societies, according to Berger and Luckmann (1969), religion provides a universe of meaning. This means that religious beliefs provide an explanation and justification for everything experienced by people in the world around them. For example, the Azande tribe in Sudan use their belief in witchcraft to explain mysterious or unfortunate events. If someone falls ill it may be blamed on witchcraft, whereas a British person might blame stress or a virus. Belief systems such as that of the Azande make perfect sense to the people who accept them and enable them to make sense of events in the world around them. Because everyone has been socialized into the same set of beliefs, this creates a sense of unity and enables everyone to interpret reality in the same way. However, Berger and Luckmann argue that it is becoming more difficult for religion to perform this function in modern industrial societies. Because there is no longer a single religious belief system, religion is less convincing as an all-embracing explanation.

Despite this, religion can have an influence on people's attitudes and behaviour in a number of ways:

- It socializes individuals into a set of moral values. Over time these may become part of the wider culture in society. Some of the ten commandments from the Bible can be seen as forming the basis of many laws in our society. For example, laws in the UK against euthanasia might be considered to be a reflection of the religious value of the sanctity of life.
- Rituals and ceremonies operate to bring people together and contribute to promoting social harmony and unity. Collective acts of worship such as marriages and christenings bring people together and remind them of their common bonds and shared values.
- Religions prescribe a moral code, sometimes through written rules, which guides our daily behaviour. We can see this when people undergo a religious conversion, which often results in far-reaching changes in their behaviour and lifestyles. Religious codes of conduct can affect all areas of a person's life, from what they eat and what they wear to what they can and can't do on sacred days.

Religion has clear links with ethnic identity. Many studies have documented how religion is important to ethnic minority groups as a means of identifying with their culture.

Key study

Tariq Modood: Ethnic minorities

Tariq Modood coordinated the Fourth National Survey of Ethnic Minorities in Britain, published as Ethnic Minorities in Britain: Diversity and Disadvantage (Policy Studies Institute, 1997). The survey included questions on the importance of religion in their lives. It was found that 67% of young British Pakistani and Bangladeshis agreed with the statement 'religion is very important to how I live my life', compared to 5% of the young white sample.

Ghuman notes that the mosque is the centre for the religious, educational and political activities of Muslim communities and these religious institutions often exert a strong influence on the way parents bring up their children.

- Religion can influence gender identity. For example, some religions have different dress codes for men and women. Some Muslim women are socialized into the norm of wearing a hijab; other Muslim women are socialized into wearing the niqab.
- Most religions have a figure of authority or worship who acts as a role model to believers. These figures of authority have huge influence on the values of their followers. Note, for example, how thousands of Catholics attended mass acts of worship when the Pope visited the UK in 2010.

Sociological theory and religion as an agency of socialization
Functionalism

According to Durkheim, the main role of religion is to socialize society's members into value consensus by making key values sacred. These values then become strong moral codes – beliefs that society agrees to socialize children into. For example, the ten commandments are a set of moral codes that have become part of the formal mechanisms of social control (as part of society's laws) as well as the more informal types, such as social disapproval of 'committing adultery'. Religion also functions to bring people together and to promote social unity.

Marxism

For Marx, religion acts to socialize people into accepting their exploitation by the ruling classes. In this sense, religion acts as a drug, which hides the pain caused by oppression and inequality and stops the workers from realizing their true position in society. It does this by providing religious justification for inequality and makes exploitation bearable by promising a reward in the afterlife for those who accept, without questioning, their suffering here and now. This gave rise to Marx's well-known statement that 'religion is the opium of the masses'.

Examiners' notes

Note how you can use examples of socialization into gender and/or ethnic identities as an illustration of the role of religion. There is more detailed explanation of these examples in the sections on gender and ethnic identities.

Essential notes

Many sociologists argue that religion is losing its influence over socializing people due to the process of secularization.

Examiners' notes

If you are asked to evaluate the role of religion as an agency of socialization, you can make evaluative comments about how parents are often responsible for socializing children into religious values, which suggests that the role of religion in the socialization process is strongly influenced by parents.

Essential notes

Aspects of identity – gender, class, ethnicity and age – are developed in subsequent sections.

Identity

Our identity refers to how we see ourselves in relation to others. It is to do with the way we answer the question 'Who am I?'

For sociologists, the identity of the individual is inseparable from his or her place in society and how the individual is defined by the culture of that society. In the process of **socialization** we acquire a **social identity** and develop roles for ourselves in our relations with other people.

Richard Jenkins defines our social identity as 'our understanding of who we are and of who other people are, and, reciprocally, other people's understanding of themselves and of others (which includes us).' In other words, identity is something that is created and negotiated through the process of human interaction. It involves making comparisons between people and therefore establishing *similarities* and *differences* between them.

Identity and sameness

The characteristics that you share with others are crucial in forming group identities. For example, someone who wishes to identify themselves as a Burnley Football Club supporter will go to matches, wear the claret and blue team colours and know all about the season's results.

Identity and sameness is also important when you meet somebody new. In early conversations, people inevitably try to identify elements of sameness, such as where they live, what their job is, what music they like listening to.

Identity and difference

Characteristics that make you different from others around you contribute to your individuality. Individuals may actively decide to adopt an identity to be different from others; for example, a boy who chooses to take an interest in ballet when his peers are all interested in football.

Types of identity

Social action theorists argue that identity has three components:

1. **Personal identity**: This refers to aspects of individuality that identify people as unique and distinct from others. Aspects of someone's personal identity may include their name, their appearance and their passport.

2. Social identity: This refers to the personality characteristics and qualities that are associated with certain social roles or groups in particular cultures. For example, in our culture, mothers are supposed to be loving, nurturing and selfless; women who are mothers will attempt to live up to this description and thereby acquire the accepted social identity of a mother. As children grow up, they will acquire a range of social identities, including their gender, class, age and ethnic identities. Socialization and interaction with others will help to define what our culture expects of these identities in terms of obligations and appropriate behaviour.

3. **Self identity**: This is the subjective part of an individual's identity; our sense of ourselves as individuals. Sociologists call this 'the self'. It is partly the product of what others expect from us due to our social identity, but it is also a product of how we as individuals interpret

our life experiences. For example, a disabled person may consider their disability to be an important part of their identity because of the way other people react to their disability. They may choose to emphasize their abilities rather than their disabilities, perhaps by competing in sporting events, and make that prowess part of their identity.

Therefore, identity combines how I see myself (internal and subjective) and how others see me (external, based on the judgement of others).

Sociological theory and identity
Social structure theories

Structuralists argue that we are socialized into our identities and have little choice in this process. They point out that our experience of socialization and social control ensures that most of us will attempt to live up to the social identities, which we adopt. People's identities are closely tied up with set social roles such as that of a father, daughter or employee. For example, if everybody sees you as a woman, but you regard yourself as a man, you may be unable to establish the identity you want. Functionalists argue that our identity is controlled by a value consensus in society. This defines and therefore largely determines what roles each person has to adopt if they are to fit into society successfully. In other words, there is a clear set of expectations about what makes a 'good' mother or son or daughter. For example, people defined as 'normal' parents will engage in socially approved ways of behaving such as protecting their children and ensuring their good health and safety.

Social action theories

These theories argue that we have much more choice or agency, where the person actively decides that they identify with a certain group. The concept of 'self' has been explored extensively by social action sociologists. According to Mead, the self has two components – the 'I' and the 'Me'. The 'I' is the private inner self, whereas the 'Me' is the social self that participates in everyday interaction. When a person plays a social role as a teacher or student, it is the 'Me' that is in action. The 'Me' is shaped by the reactions of others – that is, we act in a way we think is socially acceptable and desirable. However, the 'I' supplies the confidence or self-esteem to play the role successfully.

Key study
Kath Woodward: Identity and structure versus action

Woodward (2000) considers the structure versus action debate about identity and concludes that while there are increased choices in the construction of identities, there are still restrictions and constraints, which limit people's choices.

Examiners' notes

You will not be asked a specifically theoretical question on identity as it is not explicitly on the specification. However, understanding the theoretical debate about identity could provide you with useful evaluative points, particularly for mini-essay questions.

Essential notes

The area of identity is a useful focus for social action or interactionist theories as these theories focus a lot of attention on addressing the issue of how identities are formed through interaction with others and interpretations of our own and others' behaviour.

Essential notes

The distinction between biological and socially constructed categories is a theme that can be applied to all identities. It is also a good starting point for understanding definitions (e.g. sex and gender, race and ethnicity, age and life-stage).

Gender identities and socialization

Key definitions

Sociologists distinguish between 'sex' and 'gender'. Sex refers to the biological differences between males and females such as body shape and sexual organs, and is due to chromosomes and hormones. Gender is a sociological concept; it refers to the cultural expectations that are attached to how males and females are supposed to behave. In this sense, sociologists often talk about '**masculinity**' and 'femininity' as definers of gender identities.

People's social status, social roles, norms, values and identity will generally depend on whether they are classed as masculine or feminine. Sociologists argue that we learn these characteristics through the process of gender-role socialization.

Traditional (hegemonic) masculine characteristics	Traditional feminine characteristics
Strong	Caring
Brave	Nurturing
Assertive	Submissive
Independent	Unconfident
Rational	Irrational
Non-emotional	Emotional

Table 7
Typical characteristics that males and females are socialized into

Theories of gender identities

The socio-biological view

- Gender roles are biologically determined and are, therefore, fixed and unchangeable.
- According to Wilson, males are genetically programmed to be more promiscuous; females are prone to remain loyal to one partner.
- Fox argues that history shows that men are born to be hunters, while women are nurturers.

The functionalist view

- Parsons, a functionalist, argues that in the family, men tend to perform the instrumental tasks (concerned with achieving a task or goal) and women perform expressive tasks (concerned with affection and emotion).
- The functionalist view is that these gender roles are *natural*, *inevitable* and *functional*. They help society function effectively.

The interactionist view

- Emphasizes the notion that gender is socially constructed rather than biologically determined. For example, Lewontin (1982), a leading geneticist, said 'biological differences become the signal for, rather than a cause of, differentiation in social roles'.
- Examines differences within and between societies, as well as over time, and suggests that gender roles are not given biological facts.

For example, Ann Oakley noted that the Mbuti Pygmies of the Congo have very little division of labour by sex – men and women hunt together and share responsibility for childcare.

The feminist view
- Sees gender as shaped by a social and cultural environment, dominated by a culture of **patriarchy**. In most societies, there is gender inequality that benefits men at the expense of women, who tend to be the losers in terms of power, status and pay.
- Gender expectations are transmitted to the next generation through gender-role socialization. This has important consequences as it affects social behaviours, encouraging females to view themselves in terms of dependency, subordination and traditional female roles, such as being a carer. Women are also made aware that they will be judged by their physical appearance and this should be a major concern to them. In contrast, males are taught to be independent, assertive and dominant. They are not socialized into domestic roles and the same stress is not placed on their physical appearance and body shape.

Gender identity and agencies of socialization
The family
1. The family shapes the formation of gender identity through the type of language, toys and clothes given to children.
2. Adults model gender-appropriate behaviour, which shapes the formation of gender identities.

> **Key study**
>
> **Oakley: Canalization and manipulation**
>
> Ann Oakley (1972) shows how parents channel children's interests into toys and activities seen as normal for that sex (canalization). She found that girls were more likely to be given dolls to play with, while boys were given guns and war games. She argues that this sets the agenda for future behaviour as play is viewed as being central to the establishment of gender roles. Oakley also refers to how parents encourage or discourage behaviour on the basis of appropriateness for the sex. They manipulate their children by encouraging different types of activity – boys can be boisterous but girls must be sweet.

This concept of gender identity socialization is criticized for being over-deterministic and painting an over-socialized picture of children. Also, as Hakim points out, some males and females may be happy to choose traditional gender roles – some women want and enjoy the role of mother and housewife.

The school
- Teacher expectations of their students are often based on gender. Becky Francis found that although boys tend to be disciplined more harshly than girls, they still dominate the classroom and their aggressive behaviour is tolerated more.

Essential notes

There are various feminist theories, from liberal feminism to radical feminism, but here you should understand that all feminists believe that gender-role socialization is not natural and usually benefits males at the expense of females.

☞ **This topic continues on the next two pages**

- Subject choice continues to be gender biased. Grafton's study of a comprehensive school found that there were only a limited number of places available for members of either sex who wanted to study non-traditional craft subjects. Teachers were issued with guidelines, which required them to discuss non-traditional choices with students before allowing them their choice. Kelly found that the way science subjects are packaged makes them appear to be male subjects. The examples used in textbooks tend to be linked to the experiences of boys, such as cars and football.

However, Francis's (1998) study on the maintenance of gender identities in schools points out that not all children take up gender-appropriate behaviour – most are more fluid and some challenged or ignored them. Francis suggests that although children work quite hard in constructing and maintaining their gender identities, the behaviours typical of masculine and feminine roles are not fixed. This is because gender is only part of our identity, alongside ethnicity, class and other considerations.

The peer group

The peer group use of deviant labels can shape gender identities. For example, women may be subjected to deviant labels such as 'slag' if they adopt similar sexual behaviour to men. Lees (1986) found that females in her study conformed to gender expectations of appropriate behaviour in order to protect their reputation.

Laddish **anti-school subcultures** tend to be strongly sexist and racist with notions of traditional masculinity highly regarded.

Key study

Paul Willis and his study of 12 'lads'

Paul Willis's study of 12 'lads' in a Midlands comprehensive school found that they formed friendship groups in which the main objective was to avoid going to lessons or doing any work.

However, there is much evidence to support the view that children have already acquired their gender identities by the age of five, before the peer group has started to be influential.

The media

The media's portrayal of men and women in television adverts is often stereotyped. Harvey and MacDonald outline how women in the media are generally shown as mothers and wives. They may be portrayed as being in a panic and requiring a male to sort out their problems, or excited by the latest brand of washing powder. Moreover, even when a product is specifically aimed at women, the voiceover is usually male, on the basis that a male voice has authority and will be more likely to encourage women to buy a product. Men are also more likely to be shown in the pub, at work, or undertaking an activity. Even when men are shown at home, they are often being waited on by a women or depicted as being unable to use simple domestic appliances.

The content of media such as magazines is of a highly gendered nature. Comics aimed at teenage girls, for example, are saturated with girls dreaming of romantic love, wealth and fortune.

Key study
McRobbie's analysis of *Just 17*

McRobbie showed this when she analysed the teenage magazine *Just 17*. Finding a man was portrayed as the right way to achieve happiness and an 'ideology of romance' was perpetuated. Such magazines also gave advice on make-up and fashion to enable a 'girl' to achieve her goal of finding a man. McRobbie further argues that such ideological messages are partly responsible for the distinct cultural differences that exist between males and females.

It has been argued that studies such as McRobbie's are out of date and the media no longer presents such stereotypical representations. Recent trends in advertising suggest that it is not only women who are judged in terms of appearance and body shape. Early feminist analysis is accused of being too deterministic as it portrays women as passive recipients of the media's ideological messages – this over emphasizes the power of the media.

Religion

- The resurgence of religious fundamentalism over the past decade has played a major role in reinforcing traditional notions of female identity. Fundamentalist groups in Iran, Israel, Afghanistan and parts of the former Soviet Union insist on reinforcing traditional female roles centred on the home and child-rearing. In America, opposition to women controlling their own fertility through the use of abortion has sometimes ended in violence, with right-wing Christian fundamentalists adopting terrorist tactics to close down clinics.
- Patriarchal attitudes have meant that until recently women have been barred from serving as priests in many of the world's religions. The more traditional branches of several religions – Orthodox Jews, the Roman Catholic Church – and Islamic groups continue to exclude women from religious ministry.

However, not all sociologists believe that religion has negative consequences for women's gender identities. Holm and Bowker suggest that religious organizations that developed solely for women were the forerunners of the modern women's movement and enhance the identity of women.

Numerous writers have discussed how the practice of veiling is a means of ethnic and gender assertiveness, rather than a submission to patriarchy. Helen Watson argues that, for many Muslim women, wearing the niqab gives them a positive identity and acts as a form of resistance against racism. Leila Ahmed argues that the veil is a means by which Muslim women can become involved in modern society while maintaining modesty and correctness.

Essential notes

A number of the other major agencies that undertake gender-role socialization, such as the family and school, might be more important in creating gender identities. Oakley argues that the family is the place where sex-roles are initially established.

This topic continues on the next two pages

The workplace

- Many work cultures give off the message that the workplace is a male space. Williams (1993) argues that men defend gender boundaries at work by various means such as the non-acceptance of women's authority or sexual harassment. Blackaby (1999) points out that men create a masculine culture by displaying Page 3 pin-ups or by engaging in conversations on 'masculine' topics such as technology or sports.
- The workplace can also be an environment where the sexualization of females is commonplace. Lisa Adkins argues that sexual work has become a central part of many women's jobs. She found that in service-sector jobs such as bar-work, women are expected to engage in what she calls 'sexual servicing' – looking attractive, engaging in sexual banter, and tolerating sexual innuendo. In her study of amusement parks, she found that the more sexually attractive female workers were placed in 'front of house' roles, whereas the less attractive were given behind-the-scenes work.

These studies assume that women passively accept the gender identity imposed on them in the workplace. It neglects the fact that some women may resist the sexualization of their jobs. Also, a number of other major agencies undertake gender-role socialization, particularly the family, and these might be more important in creating gender identities.

Are gender identities changing?
Evidence that gender identities are changing

Sue Sharpe and Helen Wilkinson argue that the increasing participation and success of women in the world of paid work mean that traditional notions of female identity are being abandoned. Surveys they conducted suggest that teenage girls' attitudes are more aspirational today compared with Sharpe's study of teenage girls in 1974, where marriage and motherhood were stressed as the main ambitions.

One sign that gender identities are changing is the increasing similarity in the behaviour of males and females. In the 1980s there were claims that 'new men' who displayed some traditionally feminine characteristics were appearing in Britain. Connell noted that the 'new man' was a non-sexist, non-aggressive male who was sensitive, considerate, caring and sharing. However, in the 1990s, the sensitive type was upstaged by the rising popularity of yobbish 'lads'. It became fashionable once again for young men to have a good time through sex, beer and football. Some journalists dubbed this new style 'lad culture', epitomized by the popular television series *Men Behaving Badly*.

There is also some evidence of young females adopting masculine values and norms, especially in regard to sex, drinking culture and girl gangs. Burrell and Brinkworth argue that these 'ladettes' or 'yobettes' have adopted the attitudes of working-class antisocial males, and that the rise of female violence is attributed to their copying of the hard-drinking, swearing, confrontational style of their male counterparts. Carolyn Jackson notes that some girls in secondary schools are adopting 'laddish' behaviour.

However, the extent to which lads and ladettes represent an accurate picture of young people today is open to question. Many see these terms as being used by the media to attract interest, rather than accurate descriptions of social change.

Another area where gender identities are changing and becoming more similar is fashion. Traditionally, concern with fashion and personal appearance was seen as the province of women. 'Real' men, by contrast, were careless about how they looked, or simply followed convention. However, this is changing. David Abbott (2000) provides an interesting overview of men's growing interest in fashion and grooming. Drawing on the work of Frank Mort and Sean Nixon, he describes big shifts in the fashion styles of men over recent decades. The 'metrosexual' male, as it was dubbed by Mort, is taking a keener interest in clothes, hair and personal appearance. Their identities increasingly revolve around their dress sense, their body image and the right look.

Another phenomenon that has challenged traditional notions of both masculinity and femininity has been the emergence of a gay and lesbian subculture. In the UK, homosexuality was decriminalized in the 1960s, and by the 1970s a distinct gay and lesbian subculture had emerged.

Evidence that gender identities are not changing

Not all men are motivated by fashion or style. Heavy manual work such as mining or shipbuilding traditionally provided working-class men with a strong sense of male pride. Most of these sorts of jobs have now disappeared in the UK and have been replaced by jobs centred around computers and telecommunications. According to Mac an Ghaill, some men may be reacting to this crisis in masculinity by turning in frustration to violence, sexism, crime and anti-subcultures that are based on exaggerating masculine values. This behaviour tends to reinforce traditional gender roles for men. Messerschmidt argues that relatively powerless men use domestic violence, rape and even murder to reassert male control when they feel their masculinity is threatened by women.

The evidence from occupational roles suggests that patriarchy is still influential and that changing gender identities may be illusory or at least exaggerated. In 2004, the Equal Opportunities Commission reported that although women represent 45% of the workforce, only 9% of company directors, 7% of senior police officers and 6% of high court judges are women. Overall, there is still an 18% pay gap between men and women.

Conclusion

Postmodernists suggest that both men and women now see consumption and leisure as the key factors in defining and shaping their identity, rather than masculinity and femininity. Gardner and Shepard argue that men and women have increasingly turned to the things they buy (consumption) and do to create an identity for themselves.

Social class identities and socialization

Class identity refers to the sense of identity and status that comes from individuals' recognition of socio-economic position relative to others. It generally relates to the type of work someone does.

Cultural characteristics of upper, middle and working classes

The upper class

The upper class is a self-selecting and exclusive elite, which is closed to outsiders (known as social closure). Features include:

- a culture of privilege based on wealth and extended family networks
- a strong sense of superiority over other social classes
- subscription to high culture, supposedly appreciated due to good breeding and elitist public-school education
- concern with etiquette and social convention
- valuing tradition, hierarchy and conservatism
- hostility towards socialism.

The middle class

The middle class subscribes to a culture of suburbia based on high incomes from professional and white-collar careers and home ownership. Values include:

- social aspiration, communicating social position via conspicuous consumption
- social anxiety: a concern with what others think, resulting in a privatized and individualized lifestyle focusing on home and garden
- conservatism, reflected in hostility to change
- social comparability – a sense of social difference
- emphasis on decency, respectability and self-control
- value meritocracy and a willingness to defer gratification
- the use of **cultural capital** and social capital to encourage educational achievement among children.

The working class

Members of the working class traditionally share a common interest; they have a sense of community and collectivism gained through manual industrial work. Values include:

- a strong sense of political and social difference (i.e. 'them' versus 'us')
- traditional ideas about femininity and masculinity
- extended family support
- concern with fatalism and focus on immediate gratification.

These values still exist, but a new type of working-class value system has emerged in recent years. This is:

- individualistic, home-owning, privatized and consumer-orientated
- men may be experiencing 'a crisis in masculinity'.

Sociological theory and class identity

Marxism and class

For traditional Marxists, social class is an economic concept in that it is related to the way in which society organizes production. According to Marx:

- There are two main classes – the ruling class who own the means of production (land, machinery, capital) and the subject class who own nothing but their labour power.
- The relationship between the two classes is always one of conflict and oppression: the ruling class exploit the workers for more profit by paying them as little as possible.
- Over time, Marx predicted that the working class (or 'proletariat') in capitalist societies would become aware that they were being exploited by the ruling class (or bourgeoisie).
- They would develop a **class consciousness** and overthrow the bourgeoisie. This would result in the establishment of a 'classless' society known as communism.

Neo-Marxism and class

Bourdieu disagreed with Marx that economic differences are the only determinant of class position. He identified different types of capital (resources) that people could possess and that could indicate class difference:

- **Economic capital** – income, wealth and financial inheritance.
- Cultural capital – often related to education, this concept is about knowledge of how to 'get on' in life, particularly in the education system.
- Social capital – resources based on social connections and group membership. It is generated through networking and through relationships with different groups of people.

Postmodernism and class

Postmodernists believe that class is not a significant indicator of identity any more. They argue that:

- Identities have become fragmented and hybridized and that individuals have much more choice today about how they construct their identities.
- As a consequence of social change, there are no clear dividing lines between social classes, especially between the working and middle classes. For example, in a global economy, international groups of workers migrating to the UK change the traditional class structures.
- Class boundaries have become blurred due to the growth of consumer culture, which makes it possible for individuals to 'pick and mix' their identities based on what they consume. Identities are increasingly being based on consumer culture and lifestyle choices, which cut across class lines. For example, watching popular television shows such as *The X Factor* is not confined to one social class; it is accessed and enjoyed by many in the UK, regardless of social class.

Social class identities and agencies of socialization
The family

1. The family helps the formation of class identities; for example, upper-class families may encourage children to choose marriage partners from other upper-class families.

Essential notes

Neo-Marxists focus on developing the writings and theories of Karl Marx. Many neo-Marxists argue that capitalist societies have not developed in the way that Marx predicted. In particular, they point out that the role of ideology is much stronger than Marx anticipated and can, at times, act independently of the economic base.

Key study

John Scott: Class and social closure

Scott argues that attempts by members of the upper class to marry off their children to those who are socially, economically and politically eligible guarantees the perpetuation of an intensive kinship network and helps to promote social closure.

2. The family can promote class identity by passing on cultural and economic capital to children. Diane Reay's research shows how middle-class mothers are able to influence their children's primary schooling more than working-class mothers because they have more cultural and social capital.

Education

1. The school helps to form class identity in the way it reinforces the culture and values of different social classes. There is evidence that the top private schools (public schools) promote values of conservatism, nationalism and an acceptance of authority and hierarchy that is seen to be the natural outcome of superior breeding. Debra Roker studied public schools and suggests that students view themselves as superior to the products of state schools. She also found that they see the poor as responsible for their own poverty.
2. Education helps to form class identity through student sub-cultures.

Key study

Paul Willis: Anti-school lads and working-class identity

Willis found that the working-class 'lads' he studied were not interested in education or qualifications because they had their minds set on factory jobs. However, this did not mean that they truanted from school. The lads actually enjoyed going to school because they could have a laugh at the expense of teachers and conformist students. They did this by exaggerating working-class values such as toughness, masculinity and sexism. The school experience therefore reinforced their working-class identity and acted as a rehearsal for the sorts of values and norms they expected to express at work in a factory.

The peer group

1. Among the upper class the peer group is central, with the **old boy network** functioning outside schools to confer economic and cultural advantages on its members. The public school and Oxbridge experience is geared to life-long friendship and networking beyond school days. This also contributes to the idea of an integrated elite bound together by common cultural assets.
2. Within all classes, class identities are formed through school-based peer groups that develop along class lines. Mac an Ghaill, for example, describes different types of masculinities in a school and locates some of these ('Real Englishmen' and 'Macho lads') clearly within different class positions.

The media

1. The media encourages the formation of class identity through the way class is portrayed in television news. The Glasgow University Media Group found that the working class were often portrayed on television news as 'trouble' – they were either shown as being on strike or involved in jostling or fighting with the police. From a neo-Marxist perspective this is no surprise because the media are simply acting against anti-capitalist groups in order to maintain ruling class ideological control.

2. The media also shapes class identity through the way in which newspapers take a political position and target particular socio-economic groups. For example, until the 1970s, the *Daily Mirror* successfully portrayed itself as the newspaper that best represented the political and social interests of the working class. Some media commentators have suggested that editors of such newspapers are able to 'set an agenda' by selecting the issues that they want their working-class audience to think about and act upon.

The workplace

1. The workplace can shape class identities through the collective nature of some occupations. Traditionally, factories were made up of thousands of workers who identified strongly with each other and who were controlled by a minority of supervisors. This led to a strong sense that the world was divided into 'them' (the bosses), who were only interested in exploiting the workers and making a profit, and 'us'.

2. Many workers belonged to trade unions, which represented working-class interests and engaged in industrial action such as strikes when it was thought that these interests were being threatened by management or government. An example of this is the 1984 miners' strike, in which the vast majority of miners went on strike over a large programme of pit closures that threatened not only their jobs but entire working-class communities, which relied on mining.

Evaluation points

- The concept of class-identity socialization is over-deterministic and paints a very over-socialized picture of children. Some children actively resist the class identity being imposed on them.
- There is such a huge range of variations within each social class that it is difficult to agree on any common characteristics. For example, the middle class includes high earning, high-status professionals such as doctors and lawyers, but it also includes the owners of small businesses and, according to some sociologists, routine white-collar or clerical workers. Unlike the traditional working class, the 'new' working class, found in the newer types of high-tech manufacturing industries, have no sense of class injustice or political loyalty to the Left.
- Postmodernist sociologists such as Pakulski and Walters argue that class is no longer an important source of identity. Instead, consumption and leisure are more influential in forming our identities and these cut across class lines.

> **Examiners' notes**
>
> Theory can be used as an evaluative tool. For example, if you are asked a question on the significance of class as a source of identity, you could use the Marxist theory to support the view and the postmodernist theory to refute it.

Essential notes

Notice how the distinction between 'race' and 'ethnicity' is similar to the distinction between 'sex' and 'gender'. One concept is biologically based (sex; race); the other is about cultural characteristics and expectations. In this sense, both the concepts 'gender' and 'ethnicity' are socially constructed.

Ethnic identities and socialization

Key definitions

The term 'race' refers to a person's biological characteristics, such as the colour of their skin. 'Ethnicity', on the other hand, refers to a person's cultural characteristics. These include:

- language
- religion
- geographical origins and common descent
- history
- customs and tradition.

In the UK, ethnicity is mainly associated with minority groups from the former British colonies on the Indian subcontinent, in the Caribbean and in Africa. However, this is problematic in that it ignores significant white minority ethnic groups, such as Greek Cypriots, Jews and Irish people. It also means that differences between minority groups such as Asians and African-Caribbeans and the majority white population are exaggerated. Similarly, differences between ethnic minorities such as Indians and Pakistanis are often neglected.

Ethnic identity and agencies of socialization
The family

Key study

Charlotte Butler: Study of teenagers

Charlotte Butler (1995) studied a group of East Midlands teenage second and third generation Muslim girls and looked at their attitudes and beliefs on a range of topics and issues. She found that families are important in shaping the identities of young Muslim women. While they want their independence through education and a career, they do not want to break family links. Islam is important for maintaining family links.

Anwar argues that Asian families (regardless of whether they are Hindu, Sikh or Muslim) socialize children into a pattern of obligation, loyalty and religious commitment, which, in most cases, they accept. However, he noted three issues that were seen to be causing tensions between Pakistani parents and children in regard to their cultural identity:

- Western clothes, especially for girls
- arranged marriages
- the question of freedom.

On these issues, the family can be a site of conflict between generations. The younger generation has socialized with people with very different values and attitudes.

Ghuman outlines some of the socialization practices of the first generation of Asian parents:

Children were brought up to be obedient, loyal to and respectful of their elders and the community around them. Social conformity was demanded and individualism was not encouraged.

The choice of education was left in the hands of their parents.

The choice of marriage partner was thought to be best left to parents. Children were taught the drawbacks of dating, pre-marital sex and the disadvantages of love marriages.

Religious training was considered to be very important because it reinforced the values described above.

The role of the mother-tongue was seen as crucial in maintaining links between generations and in the transmission of religious values. Children tend to be bilingual.

Ballard examined South Asian families in Britain and found that many first-generation migrants saw British culture as attaching little value to family honour and placing relatively little emphasis on maintaining kinship ties. As a result many first-generation immigrants became very cautious and conservative in their attitudes to family life. They wanted to ensure that standards of behaviour in the family did not slip and that children were kept under close scrutiny. Ballard found that young second-generation Asians had the experience of two cultures – they behaved in ways that fitted into the culture of the wider society for part of the time, but at home conformed to their ethnic subculture. Although children increasingly expected to have some say in their choice of marriage partner, they generally did not reject the principle of arranged marriages.

Key study
Bhatti's research

Bhatti carried out research into 50 British Asian families in the South of England. The research was largely based upon in-depth interviews, most of which were with Muslims of Pakistani or Bangladeshi origin. Bhatti found that there was a continuing emphasis on loyalty to the family and on trying to maintain traditional practices related to marriage. For example, most families were keen to maintain links with relatives in Bangladesh or Pakistan. Bhatti found that izzat, or family honour, was taken very seriously, with particular emphasis being placed on the behaviour of daughters. Bhatti found that mothers saw their family roles as being of paramount importance – motherhood and childrearing were regarded as their most important role and duty in life.

Some young Muslim women are adopting quite different identities compared with their mothers on issues such as equality, domestic roles, fashion and marriage.

Religion

Jacobson studied young Pakistanis and found that they see Islam as crucial in creating their identity. It has a strong impact on their identity in terms of diet, worship, dress, behaviour and their everyday routines and practices. For many it is a defensive identity, created as a response to being excluded from white British society.

☞ This topic continues on the next two pages

Gardner and Shakur found that, among young Bengalis, allegiance to Islam was becoming more common. They argue that this is because it provides young Bengalis with a sense of support and gives them a positive identity denied by white culture.

The mass media

Gillespie notes that one way in which the media helps to shape ethnic identities is through allowing geographically dispersed communities to keep in touch with cultures that exist in their perceived countries of origin. For example, she shows how television and video are used to recreate the culture of South Asians in Britain. Some compared themselves to characters in Indian soaps such as *Mahabharata* and non-Asian soaps such as *Neighbours*.

The media also allows new ethnic identities to emerge. Gillespie found that young British Punjabis use television and videos to redefine their ethnic identities. They actively experience different cultures and mix them into new identities. This might include aspects of the American Dream ideology alongside identification with other Muslims. These new identities are sometimes called hybrid identities.

Gilroy argues that young African-Caribbeans often adopt identities based around influential media role models such as 50 Cent or the So Solid Crew. Gangsta rap and hip-hop in particular, accessed through MTV and other satellite or cable channels, have been powerful influences. The adoption of aspects of the gangsta rap lifestyle often symbolizes opposition to white society.

Education

One way in which the education system shapes ethnic identity is through the negative experience of some ethnic minority students.

Key study
Mac an Ghaill's ethnographic study

Mac an Ghaill carried out an ethnographic study of 25 African-Caribbean and Asian students studying A levels in a sixth-form college in the Midlands, where he found some teachers held racist attitudes. Later he found that in response to such racism students develop survival strategies in order to resist negative labelling. This included ethnic minority groups forming close relationships and subcultures.

Fuller has also documented how ethnic identity may be used to resist racial stereotyping in schools. She outlined how young black females resisted discrimination, forming a close group and resisting negative non-academic labels.

Basit conducted interviews with 24 British Muslim girls, their parents and 18 of their teachers. By comparing the views of the non-Asian teachers she interviewed with those of the girls themselves, Basit found some common misconceptions existed about Asian girls. For example, most teachers recognized that Islam was important to the girls. However, many of them saw it as an oppressive religion into which girls were indoctrinated. The

Examiners' notes

These studies show how education and the peer group closely interlink. If a study focuses on student interaction you could use it in answers about peer groups or education.

Examiners' notes

It is useful to be able to offer two or more ways in which each of the agencies of socialization socializes individuals into their identities. To get into the higher mark bands, you need to include a range of sociological evidence. One way of doing this is through offering knowledge and understanding of sociological studies.

girls themselves, on the other hand, did not see religion as oppressive. Likewise, the teachers thought that family life was oppressive for the girls and they saw arranged marriages as being undesirable. The girls, however, had very different perceptions. They had little or no sense of oppression – they respected their elders and any restriction on their behaviour was seen as protective, not submissive.

New ethnic identities

It is clear from many of these studies that second- and third- generation British minority ethnic groups are developing new and more fluid ethnic identities. Postmodernist thinkers have developed the idea of '**hybridity**' to refer to the mixing of two or more cultures in a 'pick-and-mix' approach to identity construction. This concept of hybridity is highlighted in the following studies:

- Charlotte Butler studied young third-generation Muslim women and found that they choose from a variety of possible identities. Some will choose to reflect their ascribed position through the wearing of traditional dress, while others may take a more 'negotiated' position. This may mean adopting Western ideas about education and careers while retaining some respect for traditional religious ideas about the role of women.

Key study

Johal's study of second- and third-generation British Asians

Johal's study of second- and third-generation British Asians, who he termed 'Brasians', found that they have a dual identity in that they inherit an Asian identity and adopt a British one. This results in Asian youth 'code switching' and adopting a 'white mask' in order to interact with white peers at school or college, but emphasizing their cultural difference when they feel it is necessary.

- Les Back has observed how new hybrid identities have been emerging among young people in Britain. In his study of two council estates in South London, he found that British white, black and Asian youngsters were trying out new cultural 'masks'. His research showed that interracial friendship and interaction was common in and around the capital, and that this produced considerable 'cultural borrowing' and experimentation in relation to music, dress and language. This meant, for example, that white and Asian youngsters living in these area were more likely to listen to rap and reggae music than, say, pop and rock.
- Gill carried out a survey among British Asian sixth-form students in the West Midlands and found that they could identify groups of students as being 'Brasian', meaning a fusion or mixing of cultures among British Asians, predominantly based on black or African-Caribbean culture. This new ethnic identity includes a 'black' style of dress, black linguistic forms and musical tastes, friendship groups that included black youths and a physical appearance (such as hair) that imitates black styles.

Age identities and socialization

The concept of age

The concept of age is rooted in biological or chronological development. In this respect we all pass through various phases of physical and psychological development, from birth to death.

Biologically speaking, we don't always have a choice about the way we behave; for example, babies and infants are not physically capable of performing adult tasks. However, sociologists point out that age is largely socially constructed, rather than being just the result of biological characteristics. There are many cultural differences across different societies and between subcultural groups, which support this view. Comparing traditional pre-industrial societies with modern industrial societies such as the UK helps illustrate this.

Age in pre-industrial societies	Age in contemporary societies (UK)
– No precise age known – Births not registered – Exact age seen as unimportant	– Biological age is a key feature of identity – Question 'How old are you' is a frequent conversation starter – Age progression is marked and celebrated with birthdays
– No clear, distinct separation of childhood from adulthood	– Childhood viewed as a special, privileged time – Children seen as vulnerable, innocent and in need of protection
– No recognized age stage of 'youth' – Young people not recognized as a separate social category because generally indistinguishable from parents in terms of values, tastes, behaviour and dress	– Youth recognized from the 1950s as a unique age group – Emergence of a youth culture based on specific teenage fashions and music
– Elders often acquire greater status and power – Elders regarded as having greater experience and wisdom than those who are younger	– Elderly not accorded a great deal of respect or status – Work is the major source of status, so retirement can result in a significant decline in self-esteem, social contacts with others and income – Consequent rise in loneliness, poverty and depression among the elderly

Table 8
Comparison of the concept of age in pre-industrial and contemporary societies

As with the concept of gender, different age groups have clear cultural norms and values with regard to identity. People are socialized into the cultural norms and expected behaviour for a particular age group. In our society, for example, we can identity four very broad cultural groupings based around age, namely:

- childhood
- youth
- middle age
- old age.

Each of these groups reflects certain cultural assumptions about how it is appropriate or inappropriate for people of a certain age to behave. Many of these assumptions about behaviour are related to concepts such as lifestyle, and people are generally encouraged to identify themselves with different kinds of behaviour based around their biological age. For example:

Youth	Middle age	Old age
Rebellion and resistance (reaction to social control)	Empty-nest syndrome	Dependent
	Financial independence	Lonely
Fun and excitement	Work-oriented	Poor health
A concern with image (linked to consumption)	Grandparent role	Retirement
	Stability	New directions
Focused on learning (education/training)	Fulfilment	Reflective
	New directions	

Table 9
Cultural characteristics and age identity

Some sociologists have criticized the concept of age identity, arguing that there are so many differences between individuals within each age category that the concept is meaningless.

	Arguments for	Arguments against
Youth	– Youth culture is just a media creation (**postmodernism**) – Most youths are conformist, conservative, share their parents' values and generally get on well with them (Davis, 1990) – Young people are not a united, easily identifiable social group as they differ according to class, gender and ethnicity – Some groups of young people resist the norm or rebel against their low status. They may form youth subcultures	– Youth is a period that is defined by growing up, rebelling, fun and excitement – Young people are all part of the same youth culture; at the same transitional stage in their life (Abrams, 1959) – During this age, young people are learning and negotiating the path into adulthood – Youth is a time for experimenting with new styles and fashion and shopping at the 'supermarket of style' (Polemus)

Table 10
Arguments for and against age identity as a meaningless concept

☞ This topic continues on the next two pages

Essential notes

The debate about whether age is a meaningless concept is more significant than for class, gender and ethnicity. Arguably, there are so many differences within age groups (according to class, gender and ethnicity) that the concept has little use.

	Arguments for	Arguments against
Middle age	– There are class differences and gender differences in the way people identify with middle age. For example, middle-aged women may be more likely to see this life-phase as about change, compared with men (Bradley) – Individuals are identified as being middle-aged by people in younger age groups. Most children will consider their parents middle-aged simply through their status as parents. In this sense, being middle-aged is more a label given by others than a source of self-identity – Postmodernists point out there is now much more choice about middle-aged identity; opportunities to stay looking 'youthful' in a consumer culture circumscribe choices related to this stage of life (Hunt, 2005)	– The majority of 'middle-aged' individuals interviewed accept the significance of signs of bodily ageing, alterations in the family structure and changes in the state of career as all indicating the onset of middle age. Of greatest importance is the awareness of a position bridging two generations – that of their parents and their children (Neugarten)
Old age	– The concept of old age is challenged by people who feel it has become a negative label, used to stigmatize the elderly – Many older people continue to drive, lead active social lives and seek to use their later years to do things they couldn't do when they were younger, such as travel	– Old age is a homogenous category and is associated with a number of cultural characteristics, such as dependency and loneliness (Victor, 2005)

Table 10 contd.
Arguments for and against age identity as a meaningless concept

Age and subculture

As part of the theory that age is socially constructed, sociologists have proposed that some age groups can be identified as specific subcultural groups. This suggests that they share the norms and values of the wider society, but they have some of their own, which makes them culturally distinctive.

Youth is an age group whose members are much more likely to think of themselves, and be identified by others, in subcultural terms. They are an identifiable social grouping, in which people have important things in common that they do not share with other groups.

Youth subcultures, for example, frequently and periodically arise in Western society. These tend to be based around fairly unique lifestyles involving symbolic forms of dissent (music, dress, attitudes, behaviour). For example, most people will be familiar with subcultural styles associated with skinheads, punks, goths or ravers. A lot of sociological focus on youth subcultures has been linked with deviance, and a range of studies of different subcultures have highlighted how they express deviant behaviour as a form of resistance and rebellion against wider society.

Socialization into youth identity

The family

- Gardner et al. found that although parents and teenagers are choosing to spend more quality time together than 25 years ago, parents are increasingly concerned about perceived risks that their children are exposed to and are reacting with increased monitoring and control. For example, *The Guardian* reported on the parents of an 11-year-old girl who were having her fitted with a micro-chip so that her movements could be traced if she was abducted. Frank Furedi argues that parents' fears are over-exaggerated.

Education

- Sewell (2000) found that African-Caribbean boys formed their youth identity in school in one of two ways. Either they become 'rebels' or 'retreatists', identities that are resistant against the wider school and teachers.

The media

- According to Muncie, youths are represented as deviant and troublesome. These representations are important because they influence popular culture so heavily. Thornton argued that the media are largely responsible for the creation of youth culture and identities. From music to advertising, there is a clear association of style with youth.
- Youth is demonized by the mass media. Cohen (1980) was the first sociologist to observe how newspapers tend to sensationalize and exaggerate the behaviour of groups of young people in order to create newsworthiness. His study described how fights between two sets of youths in 1964 (the 'mods' and the 'rockers') produced a moral panic.

> **Examiners' notes**
>
> It may be useful to study the section on youth and youth culture in an AS general textbook. Details of studies on youth subcultures (such as Phil Cohen and Sara Thornton) can be used as sociological evidence.

This topic continues on the next two pages

The peer group

- Studies show how peer group pressure is a key factor influencing the norms, values and culture of young people. Shain (2003) studied how groups of Asian girls developed distinct identities in a secondary school through girl gangs – the Rebels, the Survivors and the Faith Girls – as a way of coping with school. Their peers were crucial in who the girls identified with.
- McRobbie and Garber (1976) argue that girls have subcultures that are less obviously rebellious than those of males. They describe this as a bedroom subculture, since it typically involves girls spending time in their bedrooms, often in pairs, rather than in gangs on the street. They listen to music, experiment with make-up and discuss sex, pop idols and the latest gossip. Importantly, the bedroom subculture offers girls a chance to create a space, which they control themselves.

Religion

- Mirza (2007) carried out research to find out what constitutes a Muslim identity in the UK. One of her findings was that there has been a general increase in the perception of religious and cultural identity among second- and third-generation Muslims. Indicators of this include the increased wearing of headscarves among Muslim young women, a greater identification with a global Muslim community and a growth in the membership of Islamist political and religious associations.

Socialization into old age identity
The media

Ageism is often reflected through mass media representations of youth and old age. Advertising reinforces the view that the appearance of youth is central to looking good and that ageing should be resisted at all costs. As a result, adverts for anti-ageing creams and hair dyes are common on television and particularly in women's magazines, which also feature adverts for cosmetic surgery. Ageism may also be reflected through the under-representation of middle-aged and elderly women as presenters on news and light-entertainment shows. Sontag (1978) suggests that there is a double standard of ageing, especially in television, whereby women are required to be youthful throughout their media careers and men are not.

Religion

In their analysis of census data, Voas and Crockett (2005) note that old people are much more likely to identify themselves as being religious. There are two main reasons for this; first, a factor known as the generational effect – old people today were brought up in a much more religious era and their socialization into religious values was much more intense. Secondly, there is the ageing effect, which indicates that people become more spiritual and religious the older and more close to death they become.

The workplace

Arber and Ginn suggest that ageism against the elderly is reinforced by employment practices such as redundancy, unemployment and retirement.

Bradley notes that old people are often seen by employers as less suitable for employment because they are assumed to be 'physically slow, lacking in dynamism and not very adaptable to change'. However, the Employment Equality (Age) Regulations Act, which came into force in late 2006, provides protection against age discrimination in employment and education.

Retirement often marks the onset of old age and it can have a negative effect on people's identities. It can lead to a loss of status, self-respect and self-purpose. It may also result in social isolation and loneliness, as well as poverty and debt if a person is relying only on a state pension. On a more positive note, retirement might have some advantages in that it releases time for people to enjoy new interests, learn new skills or become involved in charity or voluntary work. Giddens refers to this as the 'third age', which allows people to continue growing, learning and exploring.

Then, as we approach death, we head into the 'fourth age' in which people become more dependent upon others as their independence is compromised by deteriorating health and chronic illness.

Fig. 3
Former *Countryfile* presenter Miriam O'Reilly, who, in January 2011, won her ageism complaint after being replaced on the programme by a younger woman.

Types of data collection

Types of data: primary and secondary

Primary data is information collected by sociologists themselves for their own purposes. These purposes may be to obtain a first-hand 'picture' of a group or society, or to test a hypothesis (a theory that has not yet been proved). Primary data collection methods include **questionnaires**, interviews and **content analysis**.

Secondary data is information that has been collected or created by someone else for different purposes, but which the sociologist can then use. Examples of secondary data include **official statistics** and personal documents.

	Primary data	Secondary data
Advantages	Data is very contemporary and up to date Researcher has more control over methodology	Quick and cheap way of gathering data Often large-scale, with large representative sample
Disadvantages	Can take a long time to conduct, therefore expensive Researcher may not be able to access target group	May not provide exact data wanted by sociologist May be difficult to cross-check findings

Table 11
Primary and secondary data collection: advantages and disadvantages

Types of data: quantitative and qualitative

Quantitative data refers to information presented in a numerical form. This data is preferred by positivists (see page 55). Some examples of quantitative data are: GCSE results statistics, the number of marriages that end in divorce and the proportion of over-60-year-olds in the population.

Qualitative data refers to data in the form of words rather than numbers or statistics. The focus is on presenting the quality of the way of life described so that it provides a 'feel' for what something is like. Qualitative data can provide rich descriptions of people's feelings and experiences. Much qualitative research consists of evaluating word-for-word quotations from those being studied. This type of data is preferred by interpretivists (see page 55). Some examples include what it feels like to be a victim of violent crime or what motivates people to join a religious sect. The term qualitative data can also refer to other types of data that are non-numerical (for example, photos or audio recordings).

	Primary sources	Secondary sources
Quantitative data (numerical, statistical, percentages, trends, ratios) Positivist (studies society in a scientific, objective way)	Structured questionnaires **Structured interviews** Experiments (e.g. media and violence)	Official statistics

Table 12
Primary and secondary sources: quantitative and qualitative

	Primary sources	Secondary sources
Qualitative data (description, words, subjective; concerns people's feelings and experiences; gives a 'feel' for something) Interpretivist or anti-positivist	Covert participant observation **Unstructured interviews**	Letters Personal histories Photographs

Table 12 contd.
Primary and secondary sources: quantitative and qualitative

The range of methods

Rather than thinking of research methods as falling into two distinct and separate categories, it may be better to think of them as being on a scale, as shown below:

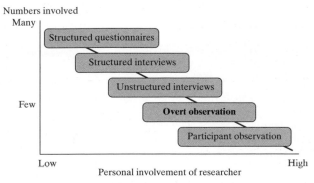

Fig. 4
Range of research methods

Linking methods and key concepts

As the diagram above shows, the more people who are studied, the less the researcher becomes personally involved with them. If the researcher thinks personal involvement is important, the compromise is that fewer people can be studied.

A structured survey researcher may claim greater **reliability** and **representativeness** from studying more people, but the participant observer will claim greater **validity**. (See pages 54–5 for an explanation of these concepts.) Those who prefer surveys argue that there is a danger of bias and unreliability in **participant observation**, and stress how the representativeness of a sample can be calculated precisely.

The participant-observer may concede all this, but would point out that it is not much use being able to produce the same results over and over again, and to say how reliable they are, if they are not valid in the first place.

The questionnaire may produce the same statistics whenever it is used, which makes it highly reliable, but it is possible that it may be repeating the same distortions. A survey can collect data only about those things that have been included in the questionnaire, and the questions may be misunderstood or they may omit crucial points. The survey style of research therefore imposes a structure on what is being researched rather than allowing the structure to emerge from the data as it is collected. On the other hand, an observation study can never be repeated in exactly the same way, so the findings can't be checked and it is therefore not highly reliable.

Essential notes

Interviews are generally seen as valid while questionnaires are generally seen as reliable. However, there are issues concerning validity with interviews and there are questions about reliability when discussing questionnaires.

Issues in the research process

Selecting a sample

A **research population** (or target group) refers to all those people who could be included in a survey. This will usually be a very large number of people so the researcher would never be able to interview them all face-to-face or even deliver a questionnaire to them all.

To make the research quicker and cheaper a sample must be chosen. The main principle of sampling is to choose a small cross-section of the research population. This needs to be representative of the research population as a whole so that what is true of the sample will be true of the population.

There are various ways of selecting such a sample. Many sampling techniques require a **sampling frame**, which is a list of all the members of the research population. Common sampling frames include the electoral register or the postcode address file.

Sampling technique	Definition	Strengths	Weaknesses
Simple random sampling	Every member of the population has an equal chance of being selected for the sample (e.g. taking names out of a hat)	No researcher influence No bias in selection	Chance that sample obtained may not be truly representative (e.g. more males than females)
Stratified random sampling	Target population divided according to the numbers of people with the social characteristics required (gender, ethnicity or class, etc.). Sample selected to reflect the proportions of these characteristics	Increases the chances of attaining a representative sample	More complicated and time-consuming

Table 13
Strengths and weaknesses of sampling techniques

Non-representative sampling

The purpose of sampling is usually to ensure that the people included in a study are representative of the research population. However, for both practical and theoretical reasons, not all studies use representative sampling techniques.

Reason for choosing non-representative samples	Practical or theoretical	Example
Social characteristics of the research population may not be known so not possible to create an exact cross-section	Practical	Sampling frame may not include research population's gender or social class
Potential respondents may refuse to participate in the survey	Practical	Some parents may decline to participate in a survey about smacking children
May be impossible to find or create a sampling frame	Practical	Not all criminals are convicted, so there is no complete list available of 'all criminals'
Focus is on gaining in-depth valid data rather than discovering general laws of behaviour. Interpretivists are less concerned with making generalizations from a representative sample	Theoretical	Just one class selected for observing teacher–student interaction at a micro level

Table 14
Reasons for using non-representative samples

Examiners' notes
You do not need a detailed knowledge and understanding of specific sampling techniques. However, it will be helpful for you to know which sampling technique was used in the pre-release material as it will give you a wider range of issues to discuss in the examination.

Ethical issues

Ethical issues refer to the rights and wrongs of conducting research. All researchers need to be aware that research can have a powerful impact on people's lives and therefore they need to be ethical in their practice and follow the guidelines as set out by the British Sociological Association (BSA).

There are five main ethical issues:

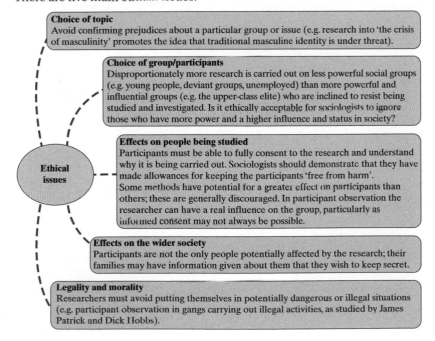

Fig. 5
Ethical issues with research

Concepts and theories in research
Key concepts in the research process
Reliability

Reliability is the extent to which a test or procedure produces similar results under constant conditions or all occasions. Data is reliable when different researchers, or the same researcher at a different time, uses the same method and obtains the same results.

For example, if one person tests the temperature of water at boiling point, then another person does it a week later, you would expect the results to be the same, i.e. reliable – as long as the data collection instrument (in this case a thermometer) is trustworthy.

A survey using a structured questionnaire tends to be reliable. The same results should be obtained, regardless of who is asking the questions. This is particularly so with regard to simple structured questions (for example, regarding a person's age or gender).

Issues for reliability

- It is very difficult to get reliable results in sociology because people are unreliable. Even with simple yes/no or fact-based questions, they may have forgotten whether something actually happened (and can sometimes deliberately mislead).
- Asking questions through unstructured interviews tends to produce even more unreliable results because responses may differ according to social characteristics and the interviewer is relying on their own interpretations.
- Likewise, participant observation tends to produce unreliable results as the observation situation is virtually impossible to replicate.

Validity

Validity is the extent to which a research method measures or describes what it is supposed to; in other words, whether it gives a 'true' picture of what is being studied.

Qualitative methods (such as unstructured interviews) tend to produce valid data since the interviewer can spend time probing and questioning the respondent and really make them think about their answers.

Structured questionnaires tend to be low in validity due to social desirability – where people give the answers they think they ought to give, rather than what they actually think. Also, people often do not spend much time thinking about their answers and the closed-ended nature of questions may restrict all possible answers.

Issues for validity

- The respondent may not act or speak normally because they are aware they are being researched. This is known as the observer or interviewer effect.
- The researcher may accidentally change or misinterpret what has been said.

- People sometimes lie, or at least don't tell the full truth – what people say they do and what they actually do can be very different.

Representativeness/Generalizability

These concepts are related to the process of sampling and how much the individual or group under study is typical of the research population.

Researchers who use quantitative data can use complex statistical tools to enable them to see how typical or representative their sample is.

If they are typical, then what is true of them is also true of others. They can therefore generalize from this sample.

Research based on in-depth qualitative methods must always be questioned in terms of representativeness because it tends to involve very small samples.

Theoretical issues

Positivism

Positivists sees the process of studying society as a science. It should involve repeating research to generate statistics, numbers, trends, ratios and comparisons that are high in reliability and objectivity. The researcher remains value-free and objective and the findings can be turned into laws just like scientific laws. Society can therefore be understood, predicted and controlled.

Positivists favour the use of quantitative methods. Their research focuses on measurement and the collection of numerical data (statistics and 'number crunching') that reflect their belief in a scientific approach. Also, by using scientific quantitative data the researcher can generate cause–and–effect relationships.

Interpretivism

Interpretivists (or anti-positivists) argue that the study of society as a science is not possible since the things in it (people) are not identical and cannot be treated as the same. To assume that they all behave in a similar manner, like laboratory animals or certain chemicals, is fundamentally wrong. Humans have emotions and passions, which make them individually different. In order to gain a 'true' understanding of an individual's experiences and reasons for behaviour, an in-depth enquiry as to why they behaved as they did is needed. This will produce more valid findings.

As researchers will inevitably interpret the findings in different ways, the conclusions may be subjective. Anti-positivists claim this is unavoidable even with quantitative data. The real aim of sociological research should be to experience the social world of the people you are studying, to develop empathy with them and to put yourself 'in their shoes' (sometimes referred to as *verstehen*, from the German meaning 'to understand').

Interpretivists favour the use of qualitative methods – their research focuses on interpreting meaning and feelings and is expressed in words rather than numbers.

Essential notes

Remember: reliability is about the method; validity is about the findings; and representativeness/**generalizability** is about the sample.

Questionnaires

Questionnaires consist of a list of questions compiled by a researcher and completed by a group of respondents. There are several different types of questionnaire with different ways of presenting questions.

Closed questions – sometimes referred to as fixed-choice questions, where respondents have predetermined answers to choose from, usually by way of a tick box. These types of questionnaires generate quantitative data and are sometimes referred to as structured questionnaires.

Some questionnaires use measurement scales – to gauge the respondent's strength of feeling on an issue. Respondents are given a range or scale of answers, for example, from 'Strongly agree' to 'Strongly disagree'.

Open-ended questions – a space is left after the question for the respondent to write down their own response. This type of question can generate qualitative data.

There are also different ways of administering questionnaires, each with their own advantages and disadvantages:

Questionnaire administration methods: advantages and disadvantages

- post: quick to reach a large sample vs. very low response rate
- internet: cheaper than post vs. low response rate; unsure who is providing answers
- doorstep: targets appropriate sample; researcher can clarify questions vs. ethical issues of intrusion of privacy; expensive
- in the street: more representative than doorstep survey vs. people who agree to stop may be unrepresentative of the target population.

Evaluating questionnaires
Advantages of questionnaires

- Practical advantages: A quick method of gathering large amounts of data, often from a wide geographical area. This can be linked to representativeness, as the larger the number of people, the more representative it is likely to be. Another practical advantage is that postal and internet questionnaires are cheap to administer as there is no need to recruit and train interviewers. Also, the data are usually easy to quantify, particularly where closed questions are used.
- Reliability: Questionnaires are more reliable than interviews because:
  - Each respondent is given an identical set of questions, in the same order, with the same wording.
  - There is no researcher effect, as no interviewer is present.

Any differences in answers therefore reflect real differences between respondents, rather than being a reflection of a non-trustworthy data collection instrument.

- Validity: Positivists argue that questionnaires are more valid than interviews because they are a detached and objective form of research, where the researcher has little or no involvement with respondents. This is particularly so for postal and internet questionnaires.

- Ethics: Where there is no contact between the researcher and researched, ethical issues are kept to a minimum.
- Measurement of trends, comparisons and patterns: Structured questionnaires are preferred by **positivists** as they can be statistically quantified and analysed to allow comparisons over time or between groups, and therefore any patterns and trends in the data can be discovered. This can lead to the development of new social laws and facts.
- Hypothesis testing: Questionnaires are particularly useful for testing cause and effect relationships between different variables as favoured by positivists. For example, questionnaires could show a relationship between social class and ill-health: working-class respondents may suffer higher levels of ill-health compared with middle-class respondents. From this analysis, researchers can develop hypotheses about the possible causes of the correlation; there may be links to poor diet or lack of exercise. Further research can be used to validate these hypotheses.

Disadvantages of questionnaires

- Practical issues: The data collected is likely to be limited in detail as respondents are restricted to brief responses, sometimes just a tick-box or check-list. Questionnaires are essentially snapshots – they only give a picture of social reality at the moment when respondents answer the questions. They fail, therefore, to capture changes in people's attitudes and opinions. Also, it is not easy to check whether the questionnaire has reached the intended participant, or if they have actually completed it themselves.
- Response rate: Postal and internet questionnaires in particular have low response rates, which can affect representativeness and generalizability. Respondents are more likely to be those with strong views on a subject and this may produce a distorted result, from which accurate generalizations cannot be made.
- Validity: According to interpretivists, data from questionnaires lack validity because they do not allow the researcher to 'get inside a person's head' and share their meanings. It is impossible to create a sense of empathy and *verstehen* through the use of a questionnaire as there is no direct contact between researcher and researched.
- Validity – lack of truthfulness: Respondents are more likely to lie in a questionnaire, or not understand the questions. They may give answers they feel they ought to give, rather than tell the truth.
- Validity – researcher imposition: Interpretivists argue that questionnaires are more likely to impose the meanings of the researcher because:
  - Questions are chosen by the researcher.
  - With closed questions, the range of possible answers has been chosen by the researcher.
  - With open-ended questions, the researcher imposes meanings by using coding or classification schemes.
- **Ethics**: The researcher is not present to enable the respondent to feel at ease or to reassure them.

Examiners' notes

As well as the advantages and disadvantages of questionnaires in general, you need to be aware of the specific advantages of the different types of questionnaire, such as closed and open-ended.

Examiners' notes

Notice the frequency of key concepts in relation to strengths and weaknesses; you should try to include as many references to key concepts as you can in the long essay question.

Structured interviews

Interviews

Like questionnaires, interviews involve asking questions. The main difference is that questionnaires are completed by the respondent (self-completion), whereas with interviews the questions are asked by an interviewer and so involve social interaction between the interviewer and respondent.

This social interaction creates both advantages and disadvantages.

Advantages of interviews

- Unlike a questionnaire, the presence of an interviewer can help since they are there to clarify any confusion or misunderstanding of questions.
- A higher response rate is more likely because it is harder to ignore an interviewer, compared with a questionnaire that has arrived in the post or via email.

Disadvantages of interviews

- They are more expensive and time-consuming than questionnaires.
- The interviewer's presence and behaviour can affect the validity of responses. For example, respondents may respond in the way they think the interviewer wants them to rather than saying what they really think. This is known as interviewer bias.

Types of interview

Interviews vary in their level of structure. At one extreme an unstructured interview (see page 66), sometimes called an informal interview, resembles an ordinary conversation, without any pre-set questions, while at the other extreme a totally structured interview will involve the interviewer simply reading out a series of closed questions and noting the answers. In this case the data collected will be purely quantitative.

Often **semi-structured interviews** are used (see page 66). These have a clear sense of direction, and they often include an interview schedule, but the interviewer is encouraged to allow the respondent to explain and develop their answers.

In reality, interviews may vary in their structure anywhere between the two extremes along the line below.

Fig. 6
Interview structure

Structured interview	Semi-structured interview	Unstructured interview

Structured interviews

These are sometimes called formal interviews and they are widely used in surveys. Interviewers are trained to take respondents through a list of standardized questions on a questionnaire, or interview schedule, with every question asked in exactly the same way to every respondent. Even the 'prompts' (extra help given to the respondent by the interviewer) are worded in advance.

This uniformity of questioning aims to create reliable data so that respondents' answers can be compared, usually statistically, to produce quantitative data.

This type of interview is likely to be composed of closed questions and fixed-choice responses. The interviewer in structured interviews is like an 'information collecting machine' who remains objective and maintains a distance between themselves and their respondents. Any personal contact beyond politeness could affect the reliability of the data collected.

Advantages and disadvantages of structured interviews

Advantages

- quick and easy to administer, therefore sample size can potentially be large
- useful for gathering straightforward, factual information about a person (for example, their occupation)
- have a higher response rate than questionnaires, which helps to produce a more representative result
- produce comparable data since all respondents answer the same questions
- training interviewers is relatively straightforward and inexpensive since all they do is follow a set of standardized instructions
- results are easily quantifiable because they use closed questions
- less interview bias than in unstructured interview as more formal (less social interaction)
- preferred by positivists as these types of standardized interviews are reliable and verifiable, and because they generate quantitative data.

Disavantages

- interviewer may have to make several call-backs to a respondent, which will increase cost
- people willing and available to be interviewed may be untypical, which may make for unrepresentative data
- more costly than postal questionnaires
- are snapshots taken at one moment in time, so fail to capture the dynamic nature of social life
- inflexible nature of interview schedule means that respondents have a framework imposed on their answers and interviewers have little freedom to explain questions
- as a result, findings may lack validity since they do not reflect the respondents' concerns
- interpretivists argue that pre-coded answers devalue the experience of the respondent (the sociologist has already defined what experiences are important so is imposing their view of the world rather than exploring the reality of the respondent)
- low in validity because closed questions restrict respondents' choices and people may lie or exaggerate, which will produce false (invalid) data
- presence of an interviewer may affect the way a respondent answers (interviewer effect – social desirability).

Examiners' notes

Notice how the strengths and weaknesses of the structured interview can be assessed by comparison with other methods. This is a useful evaluative tool.

Statistical data

Statistical data is a form of secondary data, which presents information gathered numerically (quantitative data). Numerical data collected by the government is known as official statistics. These cover a vast range of information on things from births and deaths to illness and crime. They are generally preferred by positivists and rejected by anti-positivists.

This statistical data can be divided into two types: hard statistics, on information like death and proportions of men and women, or softer – less reliable – statistics, such as crime rates or suicide rates. There are many sources of data, such as crimes recorded by the police or suicides by coroners, but the largest source of official statistics is the census. This is undertaken by the government every 10 years.

Official statistics are collected in two ways:

- Registration – for example, by law, parents must register the birth of their children.
- Official surveys – such as the census or the General Household Survey or the British Social Attitudes Survey.

Essential notes

Both the advantages and the disadvantages of official statistics stem largely from the fact that it is secondary data and, therefore, not collected by the sociologists themselves.

Examiners' notes

When discussing advantages and disadvantages of statistics make sure you show an understanding of theory (**positivism**, **interpretivism**) and of concepts (validity, reliability, representativeness) and emphasize these key words.

Strengths of official statistics	Weaknesses of official statistics

• Published statistics readily available and cost little or nothing to use
• Sample sizes often very large, which increases the representativeness of the data
• Positivists like large-scale statistics because this enables them to generalize about the population as a whole
• Surveys such as the General Household Survey would be too expensive for sociologists to conduct
• Comparison over time periods can be made because the data are collected on a fortnightly, monthly, annual or 10-year basis
• Enables trends and patterns to be spotted, which are favoured by positivists
	• May not measure what they claim to measure, e.g.:
	  – official crime statistics many not include unreported crime or crime that is not successfully prosecuted – someone who is raped may not report this to the police or the rapist may not be successfully prosecuted
	  – a student who claims Education Maintenance Allowance may make dishonest statements about their parents' earnings
	  – school league tables may be manipulated by the school, not entering some students for examinations
	• Data reflect the definitions and terms of the government, which may be different to sociologist's definitions, e.g.:
	  – official definitions of class based on occupation fail to locate the ruling class (this means that Marxist sociologists would find little use for statistics on health or crime because they cannot identify the criminality or life chances of the ruling class)
	• Interpretivists argue that statistics are socially constructed – they emerge from interaction between the person that labels an act and the meaning intended by the respondent. How one person interprets an act will be different to another individual's view
	• Practical disadvantage when the data needed may not be collected. Today there are no official statistics on body piercings and this may cause problems for researchers in this area

Table 15
Strengths and weaknesses of official statistics

Key study

Durkheim and Atkinson: Interpreting suicide statistics

Durkheim (1897) was able to use suicide statistics to identify patterns over time and between countries and then begin to understand the causes of this behaviour. However, he found that the religion of the deceased was not recorded by some countries and this was vital for his hypothesis.

Atkinson (1975) showed that coroners have their own individual ideas about what constitutes a suicide and that these differ. He argued that the official statistics on suicide are a product of the definitions and interpretations of coroners.

Government manipulation of official statistics

Governments may manipulate the statistics to their advantage and be politically biased in the way they decide to report the information. This means that official statistics may not be valid. There are a number of ways this may happen:

- The government may make something an Official Secret and refuse to publish it.
- The government has 10-, 20-, 30-, 50 and even 100-year rules that prevent the publication of data until the specified amount of time has passed.
- Data may be released when other stories dominate. This means that bad news will go unremarked. As one government advisor said on 11 September 2001, 'Today would be a good day to bury bad news'.
- Sometimes government statistics are the only source of data on a topic. For instance, sociologists cannot go back in time to find out their own data on the number of crimes or deaths 30 years ago, but have to rely on official statistics.

Non-official statistics

Non-official statistics are also used by sociologists. These are not compiled or owned by the government but instead come from independent companies, researchers or academic institutions. Companies such as *Ipsos MORI* are independent research organizations that generate statistical data, which can be bought or sometimes accessed at no cost.

Advantages of non-official statistics

- Private research companies often have the funding to survey large samples and employ a variety of research techniques, including face-to-face interviews.

Disadvantages of non-official statistics

- Anyone can set up an independent research company and anyone can use their reports. This leaves them open to the criticism that their work may be difficult to replicate and open to potential misuse.

Content analysis

Content analysis is essentially a quantitative method for dealing systematically with the contents of documents. It is best known for its use in analysing documents produced by the mass media.

In the most simple form, the importance of a topic in a media report (for example, a newspaper) is measured by the number of times it is mentioned, the size of the headlines relating to the topic, the number of column inches dedicated to it and the size and nature of the photographs accompanying the article. Most researchers will **operationalize** the topic they are examining by breaking it down into a number of codes or categories, which are then entered onto a content frame or schedule, then 'ticked off' when they are observed.

A well-organized content analysis will take into account representativeness by considering which media reports are sampled. For example, if the researcher was interested in how gender is portrayed in children's books, the researcher will use a range of books that target different age groups and both boys and girls.

Examples of research using content analysis

- Ferguson carried out a content analysis of 1970s women's magazines. Her hypothesis was that such magazines encouraged young women to adopt a 'cult of femininity' (a set of ideas about what it means to be traditionally feminine). Ferguson operationalized what she meant by 'cult of femininity' into a number of codes or categories that she could count in order to support her hypothesis.
- Some sociologists have carried out content analyses of children's books to highlight how boys are usually shown in active, creative and practical roles, whereas girls are shown as passive, domestic and as followers rather than leaders.
- In more recent years, the use of content analysis has been made a little easier practically with the use of online media. For example, Jack Fawbert, in his study of 'hoodies' as a moral panic, looked at how frequently the word 'hoodie' appeared in the media over a given number of years by entering the word into a newspaper search engine on the internet.

Examiners' notes

These examples are given to help you to understand the process of content analysis and the sorts of topics for which it is used. You will not be required to have a wide range of knowledge of studies. Instead you will be expected to refer to the study provided in the pre-release material.

Key study

Glasgow University Media Group

The early research of the Glasgow University Media Group (GUMG) used formal content analysis to research newspaper and television reporting of major events, such as strikes and wars. For example, they videotaped all television news bulletins in the early months of 1975 and then spent a year analysing the stories into categories such as parliamentary politics, Northern Ireland, terrorism, demonstrations, crime, economics and sport. They measured the frequency of particular types of news story and, in particular, examined where they were placed in the overall news schedule in order to uncover patterns of bias. Their research produced statistical evidence of the way in which TV news systematically favoured certain points of view, rather than being impartial.

Strengths and weaknesses of using content analysis
Strengths

- Content analysis is favoured by positivists as it generates quantitative data from studying the frequency of images or ideas. This allows for comparisons, patterns and trends to be established.
- It follows systematic procedures and is therefore seen as reliable. As long as two researchers use the same content frames and codes, they should be able to produce the same set of results.
- Practically speaking, it is a relatively cheap and straightforward method – mass media reports are readily available and accessible.
- It is a non-reactive and non-intrusive method. That is, the document is not affected by the fact that you are using it, nor is any human sample directly involved in the research.

Weaknesses

- The coding system may not be very reliable because it is the end-product of personal interpretation, which may be the result of researcher bias. Other researchers might classify data quite differently.
- Content analysis could be accused of analysing text out of context of the overall media report and reducing it to a set of statistics. In this sense, if researchers look hard enough for something, there is a likelihood that they will find it.
- Analysing media reports tells us very little about the effect on audiences – just because a message is promoted frequently, does not mean to say that the audience takes any notice of it.
- Interpretivists would argue that a statistical analysis cannot reveal the real media messages and uncover meanings that may not be literal or on the surface. Sociologists using content analysis may therefore miss the significance and underlying meanings of the text. This means that it lacks validity.

Essential notes

Notice how the strengths and weaknesses include practical, theoretical and ethical points.

Observation

Observation simply involves looking at the thing that is being studied and recording data.

Interpretivist sociologists use observation for observing normal social life. In particular, they use participant observation in ethnography, which is an in-depth study of the way of life of a social group. At its simplest, this involves the researcher inserting themselves into the natural setting of the social group being studied and participating in and observing their daily activities. Other methods, particularly informal interviews and the analysis of personal documents, may be used as part of an ethnographic approach in sketching out a fuller picture. The purpose of ethnography is to describe the culture and lifestyle of the group of people being studied in a way that is as faithful as possible to the way they see it themselves; in other words to 'tell it like it is'. Ethnography, therefore, is about imitating real life. Weber called this *verstehen*, which means being able to empathize with or think like the people that are being studied.

Positivists also see observation as essential, but they tend to use it more in the context of observing the results of experiments. They are much less likely to use participant observation than interpretivists.

Participant observation

Participant observation involves the researcher joining in with the group being studied.

The researcher has to decide whether to be open (overt) or to be secretive (covert).

Advantages of overt observation
- allows the observer to ask questions
- the observer can retain some detachment
- researcher does not have to lie
- no risk of being uncovered, bringing an end to the research.

Disadvantages of overt observation
- observer may influence the subjects' behaviour if they know they are being observed
- some groups will not accept being observed
- difficult to become full participant
- harder to understand the subjects' behaviour.

Advantages of covert observation
- respondents may act more naturally
- difficult to access some groups
- observer has same experiences and may understand group better.

Disadvantages of covert observation
- unethical to mislead subjects
- difficult to opt out of illegal/immoral activities
- observer may 'go native', become too much one of the group and lose objectivity.

The advantages of participant observation
- This type of research can sometimes be conducted by a single researcher without a lot of preparation, which makes the initial costs quite low.

- Researchers are less likely than in other methods to impose their own concepts, structures and preconceptions on the data.
- Researchers may gain answers to questions that they hadn't anticipated and therefore wouldn't have included in questionnaires or interviews.
- It is difficult for respondents to lie or mislead.
- Researchers understand subjects better because they experience some of the same things.
- It provides in-depth studies, which can be useful both for developing new theories and for falsifying existing ones.
- Likely to see a full range of behaviours.
- May influence group less if members don't feel they are being observed by an outsider.

For these reasons, many see participant observation as having a high degree of validity. Interpretivists, in particular, support participant observation because it allows an understanding of the subjective viewpoints of individuals. It also provides insight into the processes of interaction in which people's meanings, motives and self-concepts constantly change, so that it avoids a static picture of social life.

The limitations and disadvantages of participant observation
- It can be time-consuming for researchers, and may end up being costly if researchers have to support themselves while they remain involved with the group they are studying for an extended period of time.
- Researchers' lives may be disrupted; they may need to get involved in illegal or immoral activities, or they may face dangers.
- There can be practical difficulties about recording the data, especially in covert research when notes cannot be taken at the time.
- The researcher is limited to studying a small number of people in a single place so that samples are likely to be too small for generalizations.
- It may be impossible to join some groups and conduct observation.
- The interpretations are rather subjective as the researcher has to be very selective about what is reported.
- The presence of the researcher will change group behaviour and affect the validity of the data.
- Studies cannot be replicated, so the results may be unreliable, and comparisons difficult.
- Covert participant observation can be regarded as unethical because it involves lying to those being studied.
- To positivists, this type of research is an unsystematic, subjective and unscientific method.

Conclusion

Participant observation is advocated by interpretivists as the only research method that gets very close to real social life and therefore the most valid research method. It is criticized by positivists for being highly subjective, impossible to replicate, and therefore unreliable.

Examiners' notes

If the research in the pre-release material uses observation, make sure you discuss the advantages and disadvantages tailored to the type of observation specified.

Examiners' notes

Explaining why interpretivists see participant observation as more valid than other methods, while positivists see it as too subjective, unreliable and unscientific to be of much use, is likely to impress the examiner.

Qualitative interviews

Unstructured or informal interviews

Unstructured interviews are like an everyday conversation, but one where the subject matter is guided. They are informal, open-ended, flexible and free-flowing. Questions are unlikely to be pre-worded, though researchers usually have a list of the topics they wish to cover. The respondent is encouraged to talk at length about issues raised by the interviewer and many of the questions will follow on from what the respondent has said. Every effort is made to create a 'rapport' – a relaxed atmosphere – and to get the subject to speak honestly.

Unstructured interviews are also known as in-depth or ethnographic interviews as they go deep into the thoughts and experiences of the subject by asking very open-ended questions. Qualitative data is collected, with the emphasis on the validity of the data.

> ### Key study
>
> ### Ann Oakley: Experiences of pregnancy and childbirth
>
> When Oakley (1981) interviewed mothers on their experiences of pregnancy and childbirth she did not use an interview schedule at all, preferring an 'unstructured discussion' where the respondent could, to some extent, control the direction of the interview.

Semi-structured interviews

In between the two extremes of a structured interview (see page 58) and an unstructured interview, lie semi-structured interviews. In this case, each interview includes the same set of questions, but the interviewer can ask the questions in any order, probe for more information and ask additional questions where they think it is relevant. In this way, the interviewer has much greater control of proceedings than in a structured interview.

Sometimes a semi-structured interview may include a combination of open and closed questions aimed at collecting both factual and attitudinal data, although on the whole the questions are generally open-ended, with the focus on collecting qualitative data.

Group interviews

Unlike one-on-one interviews, **group interviews** involve the interviewer and a group of respondents – usually between eight and ten people. In some group interviews, the respondents answer questions in turn. In others, known as focus groups, participants are encouraged to discuss a topic with each other. They are guided rather than led by the interviewer (often called a facilitator), whose job is to manage the group dynamics by establishing trust and rapport in what people hopefully interpret as a secure, comfortable and confidential environment. For example, Loader et al. (1998) used focus groups with a range of citizens belonging to various age groups to document levels of anxiety and fear about crime.

Essential notes

The three types of interviews defined here all generate qualitative data, have a strong emphasis on validity and are linked with the interpretivist theoretical position.

Advantages of group interviews

- They are useful for revealing the interaction between individuals; for example, the interviewer can see the effects of peer pressure.
- They are particularly suitable with certain groups; for example, young people feel safer within a peer environment where peer support reduces the imbalance of power between the interviewer and interviewee.

Disadvantages of group interviews

- If interviewees are influenced by other members of the group, validity may be compromised.
- The free-flowing nature of a group interview makes it impossible to standardize the questions, which will reduce reliability.

Advantages of unstructured interviews

- Rapport – a relationship of trust can be built between researcher and respondents, which means they are more likely to open up.
- Sensitive groups and topics – empathy and trust developed may help the interviewee to feel comfortable discussing sensitive issues.
- Respondents' viewpoint – absence of set questions means that the interviewees have some degree of control over what they think is important.
- Meanings, attitude and understanding – the interviewer can check understanding by asking probing questions, and clarification can be sought if the respondent doesn't understand a question.
- Flexibility – the interviewer is not restricted to fixed questions and can explore any issue that is relevant and interesting; this can help build up a fuller picture of social life.
- Unfamiliar topics – unlike with structured interviews, the interviewer does not need to have a lot of prior knowledge or a clear hypothesis because these types of interviews are open-ended and exploratory.
- Validity: depth – unstructured interviews are often over an hour long so they provide rich in-depth data and can uncover meanings that would never be possible through carrying out a structured questionnaire.

Disadvantages of unstructured interviews

- Practical problems – it can be very time-consuming and therefore expensive to collect and analyse the data. Interviewers need to have good interpersonal skills.
- Representativeness – interviews are carried out on a very small scale, and therefore cannot claim to be representative of the research population.
- Reliability – not reliable because not standardized; every interview is unique and cannot be replicated.
- Quantification – open-ended questions cannot be pre-coded, which makes it virtually impossible to quantify results. Positivists argue that this method does not enable cause and effect relationships to be established.

Essential notes

All interviews involve a social interaction between interviewer and interviewee. The danger is that the interviewee may be responding not to the questions themselves but the social situation in which they are asked. This can affect the validity and reliability of interviews.

Examiners' notes

You should try always to link the advantages and disadvantages of a method to one of the key concepts – reliability, validity, representativeness, generalizability.

☞ This topic continues on the next two pages

- Validity: interviewer bias – the interaction between interviewer and interviewee can distort the accuracy of the findings (for example, leading questions, facial expressions and body language may influence the respondent's response).
- Validity: artificiality – the interview situation is not a 'normal conversation' however much rapport the interviewer tries to build.
- Validity: social desirability – in social interaction, people often try to win approval; they may be on their 'best behaviour' and give answers that present them in a favourable light.

Interviews, theory and types of data

Positivists favour structured interviews because they achieve the main positivist goals of reliability and representativeness. Standardized questions and answers produce reliable data because other researchers can replicate the interview. Pre-coded responses can be used to produce quantitative data, identify and measure behaviour patterns and establish cause-and-effect relationships. Interpretivists reject structured interviews because they impose the researcher's framework of ideas on interviewees.

Interpretivists favour unstructured interviews because they achieve the main interpretivist goal of validity. The absence of a pre-set structure means interviewees can discuss what is important to them. Open-ended questions allow interviewees to express themselves in their own words, thereby producing qualitative data that provides an insight into their meanings. Positivists reject unstructured interviews because each one is unique and cannot be replicated.

Summary of different types of qualitative interviews

	Type of interview		
	Unstructured	**Semi-structured**	**Group**
Definition	An open-ended conversation with some topics decided in advance Respondent sets the direction of the interview	Questions set in advance but with some flexibility for interviewer May use combination of open and closed questions	Interviewer may ask questions of members of the group in turn or – more commonly – the interviewer leads a group discussion
Typical uses	Used when the researcher needs to explore the world as it is understood by the respondent; in other words, when they want to uncover the subjective meanings of the respondent	Used when specific qualitative information is required, particularly when both facts and opinions are needed or when it is essential for certain topics to be covered	Used when the researcher wants to see the influence of peers or how opinions are formed through interaction May also be used to put respondents at ease – they may feel freer to express their views with peers present

	Type of interview		
	Unstructured	**Semi-structured**	**Group**
Validity	Likely to produce highly valid data as the respondent can determine the direction of the interview, so it will reflect what they see as important	Validity limited by the researcher choosing the questions and areas to be covered However, the respondent is usually able to express themselves in their own words	Validity may be high if group members know each other and feel comfortable together However, peer pressure may influence responses in some situations
Reliability	Very much a unique product of the relationship between the interviewer and respondent, so not repeatable, and therefore lacking in reliability	Reliability is enhanced if questions are identified in advance, enabling the interview to be repeated and checked	Usually quite open, so difficult to standardize questions and therefore not very reliable
Representativeness	Unstructured interviews can last a very long time (sometimes over a day in the case of life-history interviews), so samples are usually small	Semi-structured interviews can be quite quick if some questions are closed and there is a reasonably high level of standardization, so large samples are possible	Group interviews are time-consuming to set up and carry out, so sample size is usually limited

Table 16
Summary of different types of qualitative interviews

Evaluating quantitative and qualitative methods

Quantitative data and positivism

Positivists prefer to use quantitative data. This is because it reflects their assumptions about the nature of society and how we should study it.

Society, or social forces, determine and shape the way individuals behave. These social forces (or social facts) can be measured and researched in an objective way.

Positivists use quantitative data to uncover and measure these patterns of regular, ordered, predictable behaviour.

By analysing quantitative data, positivists seek to discover the patterns, trends and scientific laws of cause and effect that determine behaviour.

Therefore, positivists prefer questionnaires, structured interviews, official statistics and content analysis.

These methods produce data that is reliable (because it is standardized), valid (because it is objective and value-free) and representative (because these methods can generate large samples).

Fig. 7
Reasons why positivists use quantitative data

Evaluating the use of quantitative data

- Unlike in the natural sciences, we can never truly discover cause and effect as all the variables cannot be isolated when dealing with people and social issues. It is one thing to establish correlations (such as poverty and educational failure or drug use and crime) but it is another issue to isolate the cause from the effect: social life is too complex to be able to do this.
- Numbers and statistics cannot explain issues, meanings and feelings, so in this sense they lack validity.
- Quantitative data claims to be reliable, but it is unlikely to be so because its subjects – people – are not very reliable. Unlike the plants and atoms studied by natural scientists, people change their minds and their moods depending on a whole range of influencing factors.
- Researchers are rarely value-free and objective. Sociologists are human just like their subjects. Their values creep into the design of the research project at every stage, from which topic to study, to which method to use, to the way that questions are phrased.

Qualitative data and interpretivism

Interpretivists prefer to use qualitative data. This is because it reflects their assumptions about the nature of society and how we should study it.

Interpretivists reject the idea of an objective social reality. Instead, they argue we construct reality through the meanings and experiences we create and interpret in our interactions with others.

Interpretivist research uses qualitative data to uncover the social actor's 'universe of meaning'.

By using qualitative data, interpretivists seek to gain a subjective understanding of actors' meanings; they aim to develop empathy and rapport with their research participants by trying to achieve *verstehen* (understanding).

Interpretivists, therefore, prefer participant observation, unstructured, semi-structured or group interviews and personal documents.

They argue that these methods produce data that is valid.

Fig. 8
Reasons why interpretivists use qualitative data

Evaluating the use of qualitative data

- Much qualitative research is on such a small scale that it contributes little to the understanding of the social world. This makes it unrepresentative and unable to be generalized to the wider research population.
- Positivists criticize the use of qualitative data as it cannot provide cause-and-effect relationships and, therefore, it offers very few solutions to social problems.
- Qualitative research has been criticized for lacking validity because it is the product of social interaction between the researcher and researched. Issues such as interviewer bias and effects, social desirability and artificiality all affect the validity of this type of research.
- The more qualitative the research is, the more unreliable it is likely to be. Participant observations and unstructured interviews, in particular, are based on unique research settings, which are impossible to replicate.
- Large-scale organizations, including many government bodies, find qualitative data of limited use, as the data is viewed as lacking rigour and clarity. Quantitative data is often seen as more truthful because it is more factual and transparent.

Examiners' notes

Notice how frequently the key research concepts appear in this section – validity, reliability, representativeness, generalizability. You need to know and understand these terms as they are a crucial indicator of your ability to evaluate sociological research concepts.

Mixed methods research

Quantitative and qualitative research methods are often viewed as distinct research positions with clear differences between them.

Quantitative methods	Qualitative methods
Numerical statistical data	Data presented in words
Searches for patterns, trends, cause and effect	Searches for *verstehen* and empathy
Concerned with reliability and representativeness	Concerned with validity, meanings and experiences

Table 17
Quantitative and qualitative research methods

The divide between the two types of method is often presented as though each researcher makes a distinctive choice; either based around a desire to use a particular method or due to a preferred theoretical research position. This can result in sociologists being portrayed as fixed in one camp or another: a distinctively quantitative researcher or a qualitative one. In reality, this 'choice' is often much more complex.

The distinction between quantitative and qualitative traditions may well aid an understanding of the method's topic but, in terms of practical social research, the reality is that there is a tendency to use a mixture of qualitative and quantitative techniques as part of a triangulation or methodological pluralism approach.

Key Study

Bhatti: Asian children and education

Bhatti's (1999) research is an ethnographic account of Asian children at home and school using interviews with children, their parents and teachers, a closed questionnaire survey and participant observation inside and outside the classroom. The use of such combinations of quantitative and qualitative methods (mixed methods) has actually been the norm for some time.

Mixed methods can also refer to a research strategy that uses different methods from within one distinct theoretical position.

Key Study

Francis: Gender differences in primary school

Becky Francis (2000) used unstructured interviews and classroom observation in her study of gender differences in role-play situations in primary school classrooms. Both methods involved collecting qualitative data and so were linked with interpretivist sociology.

The multiple or mixed methods approach has generally been used in two broad ways, although the reasons for using each approach often overlap.

1. Methodological pluralism: This is where the researcher employs more than one method of research in order to build up a fuller and

more comprehensive picture of social life. For example, qualitative research might be used to provide extracts of conversations that give life to the 'why' and 'how' of various patterns and trends revealed by statistics from official reports or questionnaires. Bhatti's research is an example of this. Methodological pluralism, in essence, involves using more than one type of data to build up a more coherent study.

2. Triangulation: This refers to the use of multiple or mixed methods to cross-check and verify the reliability of a particular research tool and the validity of the data collected. Usually, triangulation involves combining quantitative and qualitative methods in order to check on the accuracy of the data gathered by each method. For example, questionnaire responses might be checked by carrying out interviews with key respondents.

Researchers will generally be flexible and select the methods most suitable for collecting the data they require. As long as the method fits what they need (fitness for purpose) it really does not matter if it produces quantitative or qualitative data.

Advantages of using mixed methods

- Adding text or narrative to numbers can help add meaning and feeling to objective quantitative data.
- Adding numbers or statistics to qualitative data can add more precision and can allow for comparisons, trends and patterns to be observed.
- The strengths of one type of data can be combined with the strengths of another. It can also allow the weaknesses of one method to be overcome using the strengths of another. For example, if participants are less likely to be truthful in a questionnaire, then carrying out some additional interviews will help identify these distortions.
- A broader range of research questions can be asked. For example, in addition to 'what' type questions, researchers can ask 'why' and 'how'.
- The overall picture can be made more valid as the data can often be corroborated.

Disadvantages of mixed methods research

- Practically speaking, mixed methods research can be costly and time-consuming.
- It requires a high level of researcher skill in the collection and analysis of data.
- The researcher must ensure that the methods will complement each other, which can make the research design process complex and demanding.
- Some policy makers prefer the clarity of one-method approaches as they are seen as being less complex.

General tips for the Socialization, Culture and Identity with Research Methods exam

The Socialization, Culture and Identity with Research Methods examination paper consists of four compulsory questions to be completed in one hour 30 minutes. The first three questions relate to the sections of the specification on socialization, culture and identity, and the last question is focused on research methods. The examination paper is related to a pre-released item. It is a requirement that this material is used when answering question 4 and, if relevant, it can also be referred to in questions 1, 2 and 3.

The pre-release material is a summary of a contemporary piece of research on one or more aspects of socialization, culture and identity. It may refer to one method or a mixed methods approach. The philosophy behind the pre-release material is to enable you to investigate a piece of real sociological research in depth and have time to assess its strengths and weaknesses, rather than being thrown into an unfamiliar research context in the examination room.

- **Question 01** is worth 8 marks and you should spend approximately 5 minutes on it. It is testing knowledge and understanding (AO1) only, so don't offer any evaluation. You get 4 marks for the definition and 4 marks for the supporting examples. Try to separate your definition from the examples, so the examiner will find it easier to award you the marks. Try to stick to just two examples, with some development, rather than listing a whole range without any depth.
- **Question 02** is worth 16 marks and you should spend approximately 15 minutes on it. It will ask you to explain two features (or ways or aspects), so make sure that you choose two distinctly separate examples. Most of the marks (12) are for knowledge and understanding (AO1), so include a range of sociological evidence in the form of concepts, studies, contemporary examples and theory where relevant. In order to be awarded maximum marks (4) for interpretation and application (AO2a), keep your answer focused on the specific question.
- **Question 03** is a mini-essay. It is worth 24 marks and will ask you to explain and evaluate a statement in relation to culture, identity and/or socialization. You should aim to spend 25 minutes on this question. As in question 2, you need to include a range of sociological evidence – there are 12 marks available for knowledge and understanding (AO1), and 8 marks for interpretation and application (AO2a), plus a further 4 marks available for analysis and evaluation (AO2b).
- **Question 04** is worth just over half (52) of the marks on the exam paper and you should therefore spend half your time (50 minutes) answering it. It relates to research methods and the question will always ask you to refer to the pre-release material. (It always starts with the instruction 'Using the pre-release material and your wider sociological knowledge'.) The question may focus on one or more methods, or on the general research process.

- To get high marks answering question 4, you need to outline the strengths and weaknesses of the method or research process using the key concepts of validity, reliability, generalizability and representativeness. Try also to refer to wider process issues, such as sampling and ethics, and link the research to theories of methods, such as positivism and interpretivism. 12 marks are available for interpretation and application (AO2a), so ensure you link your knowledge to the specific research context given in the question and the pre-release. You have had time to digest the pre-release material so the examiners are looking for evidence that you can fully engage with context. That is, why is this method good or weak for this particular topic and these particular research participants? A full 20 marks are available for analysis and evaluation (AO2b).

Notice that not all assessment objectives are targeted in each question. The explanation above provides details on which assessment objectives are being tested in each question, and the potential marks available. Make sure you are familiar with this. One common error is to include evaluation in questions that don't award marks for this assessment objective.

As a reminder:

- AO1 relates to knowledge and understanding. Relevant details may be in the form of studies, concepts, theories or contemporary examples. It should be emphasized, however, that answers which rely only on contemporary examples for AO1 marks will not score very highly because, on their own, contemporary examples are generally not 'good sociology'.
- AO2a refers to interpretation and application. The skill here is to show the examiner that your knowledge is applicable to the specific question; that you can select a range of relevant knowledge and apply it to the question set. In question 4, AO2a marks are specifically given for how well you can engage with the context of the research – what the topic is and who is being researched.
- AO2b refers to analysis and evaluation and is only tested in questions 3 and 4. You need to show the examiner that you can question sociological evidence in a critical way by weighing up and criticizing arguments.

Another common error is timing. Be aware of how many marks are available for each question and time yourself accordingly. You should aim to spend approximately 5 minutes on question 1, 15–20 minutes on question 2, 25–30 minutes on question 3 and 50 minutes on question 4.

Socialization, Culture and Identity with Research Methods (sample exam paper 1)

Tinklin, T., Croxford, L., Ducklin, A. and Frame, B. (2005), 'Gender and attitudes to work and family roles: the views of young people at the millennium', *Gender and Education*, 17 (2), 129–142

Recent sociological interest has focused on gender identity and the extent to which masculinities and femininities differ in the contemporary UK. Some sociologists have used the concept of the crisis of masculinity in relation to these issues, suggesting that men feel displaced and marginalized in the contemporary UK, and that women are increasingly taking on the roles more traditionally associated with hegemonic masculinity. Gender roles play a part in gender identity and there is overwhelming evidence that the roles of men and women have changed in the past 30 years, particularly as more women have entered the paid workforce; some sociologists have argued that there is a crisis of masculinity in the contemporary UK.

Tinklin et al. researched what young people think about the social roles women and men play in the family and in the world of work, and how this shaped their own future aspirations of work and family roles.

They used a combination of short questionnaires and group interviews with 190 young people aged between 14 and 16 living in Scotland. The sample comprised 96 females and 94 males, who were selected by their teachers (who had discussed the specific needs of the researchers before selecting the sample) according to gender and academic ability. The sample comprised young males and females of average–higher ability, average–lower ability and middle abilities. The young people were selected from six secondary schools, and all completed short, structured questionnaires before being interviewed in small groups.

The questionnaires collected data on the parental occupation and the educational level of the young person's parents (relating it to social class), alongside data relating to gender.

The schools were representative of different social circumstances: inner cities/rural, deprived/affluent and religious/non-religious. Although the schools were all in Scotland the researchers argued that the findings gathered could be generalized to other parts of the UK as the cultural norms facing men and women are the same in Scotland as elsewhere in the UK.

The research produced qualitative and quantitative data. Overall the respondents held modern as opposed to traditional views on the roles of men and women in the family and in work. There were few differences between the views of men and women in the sample, both on the roles of men and women in society and in terms of their personal aspirations. Gender was not therefore a significant variable. There were some differences in terms of the academic ability of the respondents and very little difference in terms of social class. Lower attaining females were the most likely group to want a role in life as 'helping others' (81% of lower attaining females thought this was very important, compared with 64% of higher attaining females).

Part of the questionnaire gave statements that the sample had to agree or disagree with. One example of the different statements used is given below:

> 'The man should be the main breadwinner in the family.' 22% of males agreed with this and only 2% of females.

The group interviews allowed the researchers to delve deeper into the reasons behind their attitudes. In one of the discussion groups some girls said that women were more likely than men to care for children, one girl stating:

> 'I think it may be because females carry the child inside them for nine months and have a stronger bond, so they feel they can't part with it, so they can't go to work.' (p.135)

Some of the boys thought the reason women took on most of the childcare was because the men were likely to have the better jobs and so it made sense for the man to be the main breadwinner.

Questions

01 Define the concept of 'gender roles'. Illustrate your answer with examples. [**8 marks**]

02 Outline and explain two ways in which the family socializes individuals into their culture. [**16 marks**]

03 Explain and evaluate the view that males are experiencing a crisis in masculinity. [**24 marks**]

04 Using the pre-release material and your wider sociological knowledge, explain and evaluate the use of group interviews to research the social roles women and men play in the family. [**52 marks**]

[**Total: 100 marks**]

Grade A answer

01 *Define the concept of 'gender roles'. Illustrate your answer with examples.* **[8 marks]**

This is a good answer with a range of sociological evidence, in the form of concepts and one study. Note how the candidate starts by offering a definition of the concept, which is a good strategy. Unfortunately, she doesn't quite achieve full marks for the definition as she doesn't give a clear definition of gender roles as a concept – roles and gender are treated separately. Full marks for examples are given as she clearly knows examples of gender stereotypes and how these are linked to roles.
Marks: AO1 3/4, AO2a 4/4
Total = 7/8

A role is a set of expectations attached to a particular 'social status' while gender refers to cultural expectations of each sex. Often the assumptions of gender roles are highly exaggerated and stereotypical. Archer and Lloyd defined typical stereotypes with women being more affectionate and co-operative, whereas men were viewed as aggressive and dominant. These expectations suggest why female roles tend to be family-orientated and male roles are in the workplace or acting as a disciplinarian. However it is important to recognize that the division of gender roles is less pronounced than in previous generations after moves towards equality.

02 *Outline and explain two ways in which the family socializes individuals into their culture.* **[16 marks]**

The candidate demonstrates a wide range of knowledge and understanding of two ways. Notice how she clearly separates the two points, providing sociological evidence for each one. This is a highly conceptual answer, which also achieves knowledge and understanding marks for the reference to studies (Oakley) and relevant contemporary examples (Muslim families; examples of role models and sanctions). This answer is clearly level 4, but does not quite reach the top of the band as it lacks a little depth; for example, how does the father encourage sports and discourage crying? ☞

One way in which the family socializes individuals into their culture is through the use of sanctions. Sanctions are positive or negative reinforcements of certain behaviour that can be reflected through facial expressions or words. Oakley discovered that these reinforcements were used during primary socialization to enforce basic norms and values of each gender. She called this manipulation in which the parents rewarded or discouraged behaviour that was deemed appropriate or inappropriate in relation to the child's sex. For example a father would encourage their son to take part in sports but discourage crying or apparent emotional weakness.

The family also relies on role models as a method of socialization. Role models for young children are often older siblings or parents who have been in a similar status and act as guidance for appropriate behaviour. Children will use imitation through a process of trial and error to discover behaviour that is acceptable and the behaviour that is unacceptable. For example, through this practice children learn to recognize the difference between talking politely and rudely interrupting. A further example is that in devout Muslim families it is important that Islam plays a large part in the children's upbringing; this is ensured through strong role models as children imitate their parents' religious followings.

In terms of assessment objective 2a (interpretation and analysis), the answer is clearly and explicitly focused on the issue of how individuals are socialized. **Marks: AO1 10/12, AO2a 4/4 Total = 14/16**

03 *Explain and evaluate the view that males are experiencing a crisis in masculinity.* [**24 marks**]

It has been suggested that a crisis in masculinity has developed as the roles of women and men have changed over the last few decades. As women have gained further opportunities in employment and equality at home some men have become concerned their traditional position as the dominant sex is threatened. However it is debatable to what extent the male role has actually changed and if it has, should this new status be labelled as a crisis?

Mac an Ghaill claimed that there was a present 'crisis of masculinity' due to the decline in traditional industries such as mining and engineering, which majorly employed men. An influential functionalist writer, Talcott Parsons, claimed that men take on an instrumental role as a breadwinner and disciplinarian, suggesting work is central to their identity, so without occupation men are left feeling insecure and unsure about their role within society. This crisis is reinforced by women's increasing abandonment of Parsons' expressive role of a housewife and carer for the family. Over the last few decades the female status has changed dramatically through their emancipation with legal and social equality achieved so that men no longer dominate the workplace or family life. In fact Wilkinson argues that this shift to equality is so extreme it amounts to a 'genderquake', suggesting why men may feel uncomfortable with their new and possibly unnecessary position as women become independent. Also in recent years it has become apparent that girls' results in examinations are considerably higher than those of boys as a result of educational initiatives aimed at improving female success but also indirectly due to the increased expansion of the service sector of the economy where most new jobs were aimed at women.

Some sociologists criticize Mac an Ghaill, claiming there has not been a 'crisis of masculinity' and that men continue to have a traditional authoritarian role. Men still dominate high status jobs and tend to earn more than women while women continue to be primarily responsible for childcare. Many sociologists claim women have to cope with a 'dual burden' by juggling paid and unpaid work, suggesting why women often can only work part-time, which Connell states is evidence that men will always benefit over women in employment. However, Duncombe and Marsden claim that women actually have a triple shift of paid, domestic and emotional work as they are also expected to care for their children and husbands and moderate their mental wellbeing. ☞

A good opening paragraph, which sets the debate in context, showing the examiner that she knows what is meant by a crisis in masculinity.

A very good paragraph, full of relevant sociological evidence in the form of studies and concepts, clearly focused on the notion of 'crisis in masculinity'. There is some range in terms of looking at education and work, but it would have been good to include other areas where men may be experiencing a 'crisis is masculinity', such as positive discrimination in politics, the increasing voluntary childlessness among women.

This paragraph is evaluating the view in the question. It starts off well and focused, using concepts and evidence to refute the idea of 'crisis in masculinity'. However, it loses its focus later on in the paragraph and starts to discuss female disadvantage, which is not the question.

These societal expectations of female roles have resulted in women who deviate by working full-time being blamed for 'neglecting' their children and with single mothers being used as scapegoats for many social problems. Furthermore the family continues to socialize children into fairly traditional roles with girls being encouraged into motherhood and, as they get older, accepting a subordinate role to their husband. Finally it must be recognized that domestic violence continues to exist with women tending to be the victim but often not reporting it.

While it is recognizable that the male role has changed and hegemonic masculinity is not as pronounced, it is also clear that most men still dominate over women despite shifts towards equality. Magazines like *Zoo* and *Nuts* still celebrate stereotypical ideals of masculinity such as football, sex and heavy drinking, proving that society still enforces traditional roles. However it cannot be ignored that in the past 30 years there have been many changes for women, who continue to become less dependent on and more threatening towards their male partners. While there is a long way to go towards equality for women in regards to employment, domestic responsibility and social status, it is clear that their position is gradually becoming less subordinate and in that sense we may be approaching a gradual 'crisis of masculinity' although a move towards equality cannot necessarily be regarded as something negative.

> This is an excellent concluding paragraph, and succeeds in bringing the debate back to the crisis in masculinity focus. Good use is made of contemporary examples but it also has an evaluative tone throughout where the candidate is weighing up the evidence.

> Overall, this is an excellent response, but a little too much evaluation, which isn't always focused on the question. Remember there are only four marks available for evaluation for this question and the candidate would have been better off focusing a little more on evidence of the crisis in masculinity instead of evaluating it.
> **Marks: AO1 11/12, AO2a 7/8, AO2b 4/4 Total = 22/24**

04 *Using the pre-release material and your wider sociological knowledge, explain and evaluate the use of group interviews to research the social roles women and men play in the family.* [**52 marks**]

> This is a good opening paragraph where the candidate wastes no time in defining the method in the question – group interviews. There is also some engagement with the context through an understanding about the social status of teenagers. Unfortunately the candidate misses opportunities to include key concepts, especially validity.

Group interviews involve more than one participant and are normally used to encourage naturalistic discussion on a topic rather than one simple answer. Through conversations the researcher can explore the dynamics of the sample and therefore receive a truer picture of attitudes and behaviour. It was effective to use group interviews in the study of students' attitudes to male and female roles within the family because teenagers are more likely to develop arguments when prompted by their peers and would be more comfortable with expressing themselves with a group for support than with an interviewer of a different status.

Group interviews were an effective method, allowing the researcher 'to delve deeper into the reasons' behind the attitudes of the participants towards female and male roles within the family. This is because, as a group of young people comfortable around their peer group, the interviewees tended 👉

to be more honest. The use of discussion groups encourages natural conversation where the 'reasons' behind the attitudes of any individuals can be challenged, ensuring a high response rate and improving the explanation behind answers. For example one girl offered a detailed explanation of why she believed women don't often return to work after childbirth 'because females carry the child inside them for nine months and have a stronger bond, so they can't part with it'. Also through this research method the interviewer is forced to take a role of observation where there is little chance of their bias being imposed so the findings have high objectivity, although of course another benefit of interviews is that the researcher can explain any details the participants do not understand. Furthermore, the use of group interviews in the study ensured the research was completed quickly, therefore remaining cost effective, unlike one-to-one interviews with the 190 young people. Finally it is not disclosed in the pre-release whether the groups were one sex or mixed gender. If the interviews were completed with one gender it is likely the members would feel freer to develop their possibly critical views of the opposite gender, such as the boys' opinion that 'men were likely to have better jobs'.

However there are some arguments against the use of discussion groups, such as mixed gender groups limiting the development of critical arguments against either sex as neither gender would want to offend the opposite group. Furthermore, while group interviews may promote natural debates among the participants, there can only be limited reliability as it would be a difficult situation to recreate and the answers are very dependent on the attitudes of the interviewees, which may not be found in new discussion groups. Also the conversation between the participants in this study could in fact be unnatural as young people are eager to conform to the values of their peer group so would not necessarily feel comfortable admitting their views do not fit with others or with the dominant gender stereotypes. For example, teenage boys often attempt to exaggerate their hegemonic masculinity for fear of appearing weak to their peers; this may show why they all agreed that 'it made sense for the man to be the main breadwinner' and did not question why 'women took on most of the childcare'. Another disadvantage of group interviews is that of interviewer bias even though the interviewer has little involvement in the research process. Often the social position of the interviewer can influence the extent to which the participants are willing to reveal information if their own status contrasts extremely. In this study the interviewer was older than the participants and in general young people would often be reluctant to speak openly with a figure that appeared authoritative, much like their school teachers. A clear problem with the study as a whole is that it is unrepresentative of Britain as the sample was only used in Scotland although the researchers claimed it could be generalized to other parts of the UK, and that despite the general opinion of Scotland being very traditional the students actually held very modern views. However group interviews are difficult to organize over a wide geographical sample as they are dependent on the attendance of many participants and it can be difficult to arrange a ☞

This is an excellent paragraph on the strengths of the method in relation to the key concept of validity. Notice how the candidate includes the findings of the research in an evaluative way; rather than just copying them out, she uses them to illustrate a point about the methodology. Unfortunately, references to the concept of validity remain implicit (more honest, little chance of interviewer bias etc.). There are three or four opportunities here where the candidate could have discussed validity.

This is a very good paragraph of disadvantages with a range of weaknesses being recognized. There is explicit reference to lack of reliability and a good explanation of this. However, other opportunities for discussing the key concepts are missed; particularly validity. There are some good references to the context though – again, in terms of the social background of the participants (age, gender issues) and the topic being discussed (gender roles). The candidate clearly understands issues of representativeness and it is good to see reference to the wider research process, in terms of sampling issues.

A good summary conclusion, but again, lacks reference to the key concepts, particularly validity.

location that all can travel to; this would then act as evidence that this method can never be representative of large areas.

Overall it would appear that the method of group interviews was effective in obtaining qualitative evidence of the opinions of 14–16 year olds towards gender roles within the family. The teenagers gave more detailed answers than they would have in one-to-one scenarios and had to give clear evidence behind their argument if challenged by a peer. In general the method would appeal greatly to this age group who tend to be honest around their peer group rather than for example their family. It was not specified whether the interview groups were single sex or mixed and it would have been appropriate to keep them of the same sex to allow either group to reveal their criticisms of male or female roles.

AO1 (knowledge and understanding) and AO2b (analysis and evaluation) are awarded towards the top of level 3 because a range of advantages and disadvantages are included; the candidate clearly understands what is meant by a group interview and there is some discussion of the wider research process. However, there are too many implicit references to key concepts and they are not wide ranging enough to get into the top band. Also, there is no reference to theory of methods (e.g. interpretivism), which is needed to get higher into the top band.

AO2a skills (interpretation and application) are strongly demonstrated as this response makes thoughtful and engaging links with the specific context of this research, both in terms of the relationship between the researcher and researched and also with reference to the findings.
**Marks: AO1 14/20,
AO2a 10/12, AO2b 14/20 Total = 38/52
Overall marks – 81/100
Grade A**

Socialization, Culture and Identity with Research Methods (sample exam paper 2)

Mirza, Munira et al., 'Living apart together: British Muslims and the paradox of multi-culturalism' (2007), Policy Exchange

Mirza et al. aimed to explore the attitudes of Muslims in the UK today and the reasons why there has been a significant rise in religiosity and a specific Muslim identity among some younger British Muslims.

Mirza et al. used findings from research conducted between July 2006 and January 2007. The research was carried out by an opinion poll company, which conducted a random quantitative survey of 1 003 Muslims in the UK, through the use of telephone and internet questionnaires. Telephone interviews were generally conducted in English, but in a minority of cases the interview was conducted in a different language if requested by the respondent. Some further questions were asked to 1 025 people from the general population to gain points of comparison. Mirza also conducted 40 semi-structured hour-long interviews with younger British-born Muslims, exploring their attitudes towards religion, British society and values.

The respondents were either university students or recent graduates, were of either Pakistani or Bangladeshi origin, and came from a range of socio-economic backgrounds. The respondents were selected through a non-random purposive sampling technique. This smaller sample was not intended to be demographically representative of the entire Muslim population, but it provided useful data about the complex attitudes of younger Muslims. The interviews took place in London, Birmingham, Rochdale and Manchester. Seventeen of the respondents were female; 23 were male. The respondents demonstrated varying degrees of religiosity: 13 stated they 'prayed rarely or not at all' and 27 'prayed regularly or quite often'. Twelve interviews were also conducted with non-Muslims of similar age to provide points of possible comparison. The interviews were transcribed and then analysed using computer-assisted data analysis software.

Mirza found that Muslim identity in the UK is more contradictory and complex than it first appears. The majority of Muslims strongly identify their religion as being important to them. Nearly half pray five times a day and 86% of respondents also believed that their religion was the most important thing in their life. When asked the same question, only 11% of the wider British population felt the same. One driving factor behind rising religiosity among young British Muslims is anger about Western foreign policy, particularly in relation to Afghanistan and Iraq. In this sense, the turn to religion might be understood as an expression of solidarity with other Muslims around the world. Another, more long-term, factor in the rise of a specifically Muslim identity is the decline of many older forms of identity in UK society in the last two decades – for instance, those established through political parties, trade unions and nationhood. This means that people are turning to other ways to search for meaning and belonging, which might include their religion. Younger Muslims are more likely than their parents to feel a connection to their religious community as opposed to their county or ethnic group or a political party. Whereas the first Muslim immigrants to the UK adapted their customs to fit Western lifestyles, their children today are more willing to express their own religious identity publicly. For example, an increasing number of young Muslim women choose to wear the full hijab (headscarf) as an expression of their religious faith, and younger British Muslims are also more likely to state a preference for living under Sharia law. Responses towards women wearing the veil were:

I prefer that Muslim women choose to wear the veil (53%)

I prefer that Muslim women choose not to wear the veil (28%)

Don't know/refused to answer (19%)

Questions

01 Define the concept of 'cultural diversity'. Illustrate your answer with examples. [**8 marks**]

02 Outline and explain two ways in which individuals learn society's culture. [**16 marks**]

03 Explain and evaluate the view that religion is an important source of identity to British minority ethnic groups today. [**24 marks**]

04 Using the pre-release material and your wider sociological knowledge, explain and evaluate the use of mixed methods in researching the attitudes of Muslims in Britain today. [**52 marks**]

[**Total: 100 marks**]

Grade C answer

01 *Define the concept of 'cultural diversity'. Illustrate your answer with examples.* **[8 marks]**

'Cultural diversity' refers to the differences between groups regarding values and norms that exist in a particular region or in the world. In recent years cultural diversity has become the norm with an increase in subcultures, a group within a national culture that have specific behaviour or beliefs. This increasing diversity exists within all areas of society so most individuals are members of numerous subcultures. These groups can be categorized by class, region, age, sexuality and most predominantly ethnicity with the increasing aspect of multiculturalism in modern-day society as individuals subscribe to British culture while maintaining their commitments to their mother culture.

The definition demonstrates full core meaning. The first sentence offers an accurate definition and this is followed by some wider explanation. The examples are less clear. There are several examples of sub-cultural groups but these needed to be developed further in terms of cultural diversity. For example, the student could have given examples of 'commitment to the mother culture'.
Marks: AO1 4/4, AO2a 2/4
Total = 6/8

02 *Outline and explain two ways in which individuals learn society's culture.* **[16 marks]**

One way in which individuals learn society's culture is through the use of sanctions, encouragement and discouragement by others of their behaviour. Sanctions act as a key technique of primary socialization with parents reinforcing or rewarding appropriate behaviour and punishing 'naughty' behaviour. This early process acts to develop children's conscience as they begin to recognize the difference between 'good' and 'bad' as well as acknowledging the consequence of their actions. Morgan claimed toilet-training relied on sanctions as children realize that control over bodily functions can lead to acceptance into wider society. Sanctions are used in the construction of gender identity with Oakley's claims that parents use manipulation to establish sex-appropriate behaviour.

Another way in which individuals are socialized into their surrounding culture is through their imitation of people who already follow the norms and values of their society, otherwise referred to as role models. Role models are used in the media, which is becoming increasingly more influential with images and ideas used to indicate how the public should fashion their lifestyles. For example, David and Victoria Beckham are role models to young people in terms of fashion. They set the style and everyone follows. Alan Sugar is in the media a lot and he is a role model for people wanting to be successful in business.

Two ways are explicit and accurate with some sociological evidence in terms of concepts and studies. This takes it to level 3 of the mark scheme for AO1 (knowledge and understanding). It doesn't reach level 4 because it is underdeveloped in terms of range and depth of knowledge. For example, it would have been better to have some explanation of what Oakley meant by manipulation, maybe with some illustrative examples. It is also imbalanced – the first way is stronger than the second with more sociological concepts and studies. The examples offered in the second paragraph lack support from sociological evidence and are not explicitly focusing on the learning of society's ☞

culture. In terms of AO2a skills (interpretation and application), this response is reasonably well focused on how individuals learn their culture, but there is not enough selection of a range of evidence for the top mark.
**Marks: AO1 8/12, AO2a 3/4
Total = 11/16**

This is a good introduction, which scores AO2a marks as it explicitly focuses on religion and sets the question within a wider social context.

This paragraph focuses on reasons why minority ethnic groups may be more religious, but notice that the question is about contemporary society and this candidate needs to be aware that Weber's and Durkheim's theories need a more explicit connection with today's society.

Notice how this paragraph is much more contemporary, which clearly addresses the question. There are explicit references to sociological studies and concepts, which lifts this to be at least a level 3 answer.

This is explicit evaluation of the view in the question, but it is narrow as it is one well developed point, with a good use made of sociological language.

03 *Explain and evaluate the view that religion is an important source of identity to British minority ethnic groups today.* **[24 marks]**

Ethnic minority groups account for 8% of the population massively outnumbered by the white British group who dominate all areas of national culture. While the predominant British religion is Christianity other religions have been introduced through the arrival of immigrants over the last few decades. The Home Office survey of the nation's beliefs found clear evidence that all ethnic minority groups valued religion more highly than white Christians, fuelling the debate of how significant religion is in the identities of minority groups.

Ethnic minorities tend to have a greater religious following than the long-established and increasingly secularized population. Weber suggested that members of deprived groups were more religious through seeking an explanation for their disadvantage and their hope of salvation. Durkheim went further to suggest the religion of immigrants bonded new communities through shared norms and values of rituals such as the established African-Caribbean Christian community, which has adopted an evangelical affiliation emphasizing conversation and accuracy of the Bible.

These black-led churches developed through the rejection of their members from existing Christian churches and Bird claimed they still act as institutions that enable their follower to cope with and adjust to racist and unjust society while Beckford suggested this style of Christianity offers black people a sense of hope and independence in their often poor social status. These churches have had a massive following in Britain reflected through their increase, with half of the churches started since 1998 being ethnic-minority institutions, particularly black churches.

On the other hand some sociologists argue that religion is a limited source of identity for ethnic minorities in Britain. It has been claimed that over the years religion has become less important to ethnic minorities as the later generations become more engaged with British culture and secularization. The attendance of under 20s to religious temples has declined more than any other age category with the least religiously committed being the Sikhs.

This is a level 3 answer for all assessment objectives. In terms of knowledge and understanding, this response is clearly more than basic as it contains some accurate sociological evidence, using concepts, studies and contemporary examples. However, it lacks in range of evidence and in this sense, it is a little brief. For example, this response is almost exclusively focused on black African-Caribbean identity, which is only one minority ethnic group. In terms of evaluation, there is some explicit evaluation but it is narrowly focused.
Marks: AO1 9/12, AO2a 5/8, AO2b 3/4 Total = 17/24

---

04 *Using the pre-release material and your wider sociological knowledge, explain and evaluate the use of mixed methods in researching the attitudes of Muslims in Britain today.* **[52 marks]**

The experiment used semi-structured interviews and telephone and internet questionnaires to gain information about the attitudes of Muslims in Britain today. The use of mixed methods offers a combination of quantitative and qualitative data, which as a result produce numerous advantages and disadvantages.

This is a confusing start with the mention of experiment. The term experiment is a research method, which was not used in this study.

The use of mixed methods in researching the attitudes of Muslims in Britain today is effective because it ensures all disadvantages of quantitative or qualitative methods are counter acted. The data collected was predominantly from the telephone and internet questionnaires of over 2000 individuals producing quantitative data that could easily be analysed although the qualitative findings of the semi-structured interviews of 40 young Muslims was also effectively examined with computer-assisted data analysis software. The questionnaires were taken by around a 50/50 split of Muslims and the general population to allow the attitudes of the participant Muslims to be directly compared with others to distinguish any noticeable differences. The questionnaire evidence was representative of Muslims in the UK due to the large sample size, so effective generalizations could be defined about Muslim attitudes. Furthermore the semi-structured interviews with younger Muslim students were representative of the age group with the participants from a range of different socio-economic backgrounds.

This paragraph starts off being heavily descriptive and the candidate must be careful not to end up copying out chunks of the pre-release. There is a practical focus without many links to research concepts in the first half of the paragraph. However, this improves with references to representativeness and generalizability.

The semi-structured interviews also ensured that while offering a valid picture of the complex opinions of younger Muslims the methods also remained reliable. The limited use of vaguely structured interviews with only 40 participants and the internet and telephone questionnaires ensured that the experiment was not as time-consuming as a large sample of unstructured interviews, so costs were kept down and the answers received were directly linked to the topics without going off the point.

However the combination of quantitative and qualitative methods can also cause problems with the individual advantages being threatened or cancelled out. For example, while strong validity is offered through the interviews the overall validity of the results are lowered because the majority of the ☞

The key concepts of validity and reliability are used accurately, but are not developed. The candidate needs to explain why they are valid and why they are reliable. This is followed by a heavy reliance on practical issues, unrelated to any key concepts.

This is quite a good paragraph with a range of weaknesses of using mixed methods. There is an accurate discussion of key concepts, such as validity, but again they are underdeveloped. Why does quantitative data lower validity? There is also a missed opportunity to talk about validity in terms of interviewer effects and 'one word responses'. Overall, the key concepts in this paragraph are either implicit or underdeveloped.

This summary doesn't really add any substance to the response as it is just a summary. There are no more key concepts discussed in any depth and the context referred to is given no more than lip service.

data was quantitative. Also the method of semi-structured interviews can also be limiting because the interviewer may have an effect on the interviewee. Another issue of combining interview and questionnaire findings is that although it has become easier to analyse qualitative data through computer programmes, as used in the study it is very difficult to compare qualitative opinions and feelings and quantitative one-word responses or numbers, so the conclusion of Muslim attitudes may not be completely accurate. Furthermore the method of questionnaires via phone calls and over the internet have low response rates or engagement with participants being unlikely to be bothered with answering questions choosing quick and undetailed responses. The representative nature of the large sample of questionnaires is threatened by the weakness of the interviews, which were only completed with a small group of participants.

Overall, the combination of questionnaires and interviews offers an in-depth picture of Muslim attitudes with a mix of qualitative and quantitative data and can improve the weaknesses that each method suffers from. Mixed methods ensures that the range and depth of information is increased with basic closed answers about a wide array of topics and more specific but less general opinions of Muslims. However the advantages of qualitative and quantitative methods tend to be opposing so the use of mixed methods can cancel out the positive effects of factors such as reliability, validity, representativeness etc.

This response is a lower level 3 answer for AO1 and AO2b. There are a range of strengths and weaknesses discussed, with some reference to the wider research process, particularly in terms of sampling. However, there is a lack of range and depth in terms of key methodological concepts, such as validity and reliability. In terms of AO2a, the candidate does make many references to Muslims but doesn't engage in any depth with the context of the research. The reference to Muslim attitudes is, in many cases, no more than lip service, which means that any group of people could have been inserted, such as white British, or elderly people. To engage with the context, you need to think about the strengths and weaknesses in terms of this particular group and this particular topic: what is good and problematic about using mixed methods to study the particular group of minority ethnic Muslims about their attitudes in Britain today?

Marks: AO1 11/20 AO2a 6/12 AO2b 11/20 Total = 28/52
Overall marks – 62/100
Grade C

Improving your grade

The following examples show how you can improve your response to a short answer question.

01 *Define the concept of 'popular culture'. Illustrate your answer with examples.* **[8 marks]**

Weak answer

Popular culture is looked down on by the middle and upper classes who prefer opera and ballet. The products of the mass media like *The X Factor* are seen as examples of popular culture.

In terms of the definition, there is no core meaning given here although 2 marks are picked up for links to upper classes and mass media and 1 mark for *The X Factor* as a partial example only, since it doesn't explain why this is an example of popular culture.
Marks: 3/8

Better answer

Popular culture refers to the way of life of the mass of the population. It is often looked down on by the middle and upper class followers of 'high culture' such as opera and ballet. The products of the mass media are often seen as examples of popular culture. *The X Factor* for example is followed by many millions of 'ordinary' people but often looked down on and regarded as inferior by the middle and upper classes.

This answer is awarded full marks for the definition but only provides one full example, which is awarded 2 marks.
Marks: 6/8

Good answer

Popular culture refers to the way of life and, in particular, the preferred leisure activities of the mass of the population. It is often looked down on by the middle- and upper-class followers of 'high culture' such as opera and ballet. The products of the mass media are often seen as examples of popular culture. *The X Factor* for example is followed by many millions of 'ordinary' people but often looked down on and regarded as inferior by the middle and upper classes. Football used to be an important part of popular culture for many working-class men, although today it has become so expensive to watch top-class football that it is beyond the financial means of many ordinary people.

This is awarded four marks for the definition as it includes core meaning (reference to way of life of the masses) and some development (contrasting with high culture and link to mass media). This gets full marks also for the examples of *The X Factor* and football, both of which are explained in terms of popular culture.
Marks: 8/8

Socialization, Culture and Identity with Research Methods

Achieved status	Status, which is gained by the individual through talent, hard work and effort
Anticipatory socialization	A concept referring to workplace socialization where people may have learned about a new job beforehand
Anti-school subculture	A set of norms and values that goes against the established rules and expectations of the school. It may form because students feel that they are not valued by the school or because they do not identify with the value system and goals of the school
Ascribed status	Status, which is fixed and determined at birth
Canalization	Directing children's interests into certain toys and play activities; particularly relevant for gender-role socialization
Class consciousness	A shared awareness held by members of a social class that they subscribe to a common set of conditions
Collective conscience	The shared ways of thinking and shared moral beliefs of a society
Commodification	A Marxist concept referring to capitalist societies where products increasingly become commodities – things that can be bought and sold
Commodity fetishism	A Marxist concept referring to the idea that in capitalist societies, people worship consumer commodities
Conspicuous consumption	Buying of particular brands, logos and designer goods as status symbols
Consumer culture	Related to the goods and services we buy and consume in society
Content analysis	A research method that involves identifying a set of categories and systematically counting the frequency with which each category occurs within a given area of the media
Covert observation	Where the researcher does not inform the people being researched of the true nature of their role
Culture	The learned and shared 'way of life' of any society
Cultural capital	Often related to education, knowledge of how to 'get on' in life, particularly in the education system. It is a concept used by neo-Marxists and is associated with the middle and upper classes
Cultural diversity	Cultural differences within a society. It links to the idea of subcultures because the existence of different subcultures leads to a culturally diverse society
Economic capital	Income, wealth and financial inheritance
Ethics	The rights and wrongs of doing research. Social scientists must adhere to a code of ethics, which includes guiding principles such as protecting participants from harm and ensuring confidentiality and anonymity
Ethnicity	A person's cultural characteristics, which include language, religion, geographical origins and common descent, history, customs and traditions
Femininity	The characteristics and behaviour patterns that have traditionally been defined as socially appropriate for females
Feminism	A set of theories that aim to explain the position of women in society

Feral children	Children who have grown up with limited human contact
Formal curriculum	The official curriculum; what governments specify children need to learn and be taught through lessons in school
Formal social control	Mechanisms of social control, which involve written rules, laws or codes of conduct that individuals need to follow
Formal socialization	Refers to workplace socialization where official ways of socializing workers are used; for example, the management of a company may provide training courses
Functionalism	A sociological theory that sees societies as characterized by social order and consensus or agreement
Gender roles	The cultural expectations that are attached to how males and females are supposed to behave – sociologists often talk about 'masculinity' and 'femininity' as definers of gender identities
Generalizability	If a sample is representative, then the findings can be applied to the wider research population
Global culture	The idea that due to the development of social and economic relationships on a global scale, we are all becoming part of one, all-embracing culture. In other words, people all around the world will share a similar way of life
Group interview	An interview where a group (usually between 8 and 10 people) are interviewed together. Sometimes, the respondents answer questions in turn. In **focus groups** participants are encouraged to discuss a topic with each other while the interviewer acts as a facilitator
Hidden curriculum	Also known as the informal curriculum, this refers to the transmission of norms and values, which are not part of the formal or official curriculum
High culture	The cultural practices, which are associated with the powerful and wealthy elite or upper social classes
Hybridity or hybrid culture	A coming together or fusion of cultures, styles and identities resulting in the formation of new ones
Identity	Our sense of who we are and how we see ourselves in relation to others
Ideology	The ideas of the ruling class, which help to legitimate and justify the existing economic system
Imitation	Copying the behaviour of others; often used to describe gender-role socialization
Informal social control	The unwritten, more informal ways of controlling people that are learnt during everyday interactions
Informal socialization	Refers to the workplace where socialization is provided by peer groups at work who introduce new workers to the informal culture of the workplace
Interactionism	(Also referred to as social action theories.) A sociological theory, which sees individuals as creative actors who interpret society through their interactions with others
Interpretivism	Sometimes referred to as anti-positivism, the view that sociologists cannot study society scientifically as individuals are complex and unique. Favours methods that emphasize *verstehen* and validity and which produce qualitative data that explores the interpretation of the world held by the research subjects

Manipulation	The way in which parents encourage and reward behaviour, which they think is appropriate and discourage that which they think is inappropriate
Marxism	A sociological theory that sees society as being characterized by class inequality, exploitation and conflict
Masculinity	The characteristics and behaviour patterns that have been traditionally defined as socially appropriate for males
Multiculturalism	The promotion of cultural diversity, specifically related to different ethnic cultures existing side by side where each group has the right to preserve their own cultural heritage
Nature–nurture debate	The debate about whether human behaviour is biologically based on instinct (nature) or whether it is socially learned (nurture)
Non-official statistics	Numerical data that is compiled and owned by independent research companies such as market research organizations, rather than the government
Non-participant observation	Observation where the sociologist does not join in the activities of the group they are researching
Norms	Social rules, which define the acceptable and expected ways of behaving in a given social situation
Official statistics	Numerical data collected by the government
Old boy network	The informal network of contacts, support and services offered by ex-public schoolboys to each other, especially those who attended the same school
Operationalize	To define something in such a way that it can be measured
Overt observation	Observation where research participants know that they are being researched
Participant observation	Observation where the researcher joins in with the group being studied
Patriarchy	A system of male domination
Peer groups	People of a similar status who come into regular contact with each other, for example, groups of friends, school children in the same year or colleagues in the same job
Peer group pressure	The influence that peer groups have on their members to imitate group behaviour. Belonging to and being accepted by a peer group are powerful forces, which encourage people to conform to the group for fear of not fitting in
Personal identity	Aspects of individuality that identify people as unique and distinct from others
Primary socialization	The earliest stages of socialization, beginning at birth and continuing through the early years of life. Most primary socialization takes places within the family with people in a child's life with whom they have primary (close, personal, intimate and face-to-face) relationships
Popular culture	The activities enjoyed by the masses, or the vast majority of ordinary people
Postivism	An approach to studying society, which uses the methodology of the natural sciences. It favours certain methods (e.g. the structured questionnaire) that are seen as emphasizing the scientific characteristics of reliability, objectivity and quantitative data

Postmodernism	A sociological theory, which criticizes early sociological theories as being outdated and inapplicable to a postmodern world
Primary data	Information collected by sociologists themselves for their own purpose
Qualitative data	Information that is non-numerical, usually in the form of words (but also images and audio recordings). It concentrates on presenting the quality of the way of life described rather than on presenting statistics; it focuses on giving a 'feel' for what something is like
Quantitative data	Information in a numerical form
Questionnaires	A type of survey, which consist of lists of questions compiled by the researcher and completed by the respondent
Random sampling	Where each member of the sample frame has an equal chance of being selected for the sample
Reliability	The extent to which a test or procedure produces similar results under constant conditions or all occasions. Data is reliable when different researchers, or the same researcher at a different time, uses the same method and obtains the same results
Representativeness	How far the individual or group under study is typical of the research population
Research population	All the people who could be included in some research
Re-socialization	A concept referring to workplace socialization. When individuals start a new place of work they have to learn new rules, regulations and norms of behaving, such as submitting to workplace discipline
Roles	Patterns of behaviour, which are expected of a person or group of people relating to their position in society
Role models	A significant other, such as a parent, upon whom others, especially young people, may model their behaviour and beliefs
Ruling class	A Marxist concept which refers to the class who own the means of production in any society (e.g. land, capital, machinery)
Sanctions	The rewards and punishments by which social control is achieved and conformity to norms and values enforced. These may be either positive sanctions, which are rewards, or negative sanctions, which are punishments
Sampling frame	A list of all the members of the research population
Secondary data	Information that has been collected or created by someone else for their own purposes, but which the sociologist can then use
Secondary socialization	The socialization that occurs between the individual and those people in their life with whom they have secondary relationships. Secondary socialization functions to build on what has been learned in primary socialization in order for children to understand and participate in the wider society, beyond their immediate family
Self identity	The subjective part of an individual's identity; a sense of ourselves as individuals
Semi-structured interview	Research where each interview includes the same set of questions, but the interviewer can ask the questions in any order, probe for more information and ask additional questions where they think it is relevant

Social class	A group of people who share a similar socio-economic position in terms of occupation, income, ownership of wealth and, generally, similar levels of education, status and lifestyle
Social closure	The ability of the upper class to close themselves off from lower social classes and stop them from moving upwards into their ranks
Social construction	Defined by the norms and values of a society, rather than being biologically determined
Social control	The term given to the various methods used to persuade or force individuals to conform to the dominant social norms and values of a society
Social identity	The personality characteristics and qualities that particular cultures associate with certain social roles or groups
Social structure theories	Theories that see our behaviour as constrained and determined by society
Socialization	The process of learning society's culture
Stratified sampling	Involves dividing the target population according to the numbers of people with the social characteristics required, such as gender, ethnicity or class and then selecting the sample to reflect the proportions of these characteristics
Structured interviews	A type of survey that has a fixed schedule of questions, in which answers are recorded by an interviewer
Subculture	A minority part of the majority culture where members are committed to the wider culture that dominates society but they have distinct norms and values, which make them different and distinctive
Subject class	A Marxist concept, which means the social class who are exploited in society because they own nothing, except their ability to work and earn a wage
Statistical data	A form of secondary data, which presents data gathered numerically (quantitative data)
Status	A concept used in two main ways: it can refer to the social position of people in society (such as a mother or a worker) or it can refer to the ranking of individuals, which is determined by the prestige or respect attached to their position, as given by other members of society
Unstructured interviews	Informal, open-ended, flexible and free-flowing interviews. Questions are unlikely to be pre-worded though researchers usually have a list of the topics they wish to cover
Validity	The extent to which a research method measures or describes what it is supposed to. In other words, when it gives a 'true' picture of what is being studied
Values	General principles or beliefs about what is desirable and worthwhile
Value consensus	Shared agreement about what is worthwhile and desirable